BEXHILL-ON-SEA

A HISTORY

Pen and ink drawing of St Peter's church by Charles Graves. The drawing was perhaps made around 1900, based on a photograph showing the church before 1878. Note the children on the path and the man on the roof.

BEXHILL-ON-SEA
A HISTORY

Julian Porter

Phillimore

First published 2004, this edition 2015

Phillimore & Co. Ltd, an imprint of The History Press
The Mill, Brimscombe Port
Stroud, Gloucestershire, GL5 2QG
www.thehistorypress.co.uk

British Library Cataloguing in Publication Data.
A catalogue record for this book is available from the British Library.

ISBN 978 0 7509 6736 5

Typesetting and origination by The History Press
Printed and bound in Great Britain by
Marston Book Services Ltd, Oxfordshire

CONTENTS

Dedicated to my parents

This book has been compiled from the archives and collections of Bexhill Museum

LIST OF ILLUSTRATIONS

Frontispiece: Pen and ink drawing of St Peter's church

ACKNOWLEDGEMENTS

This book would not have been possible without the assistance and knowledge of William Hedger and Mary Hart. Their research, suggestions, corrections and proofreading were invaluable and I am greatly indebted to them.

I must also thank Don Phillips for his research, help and assistance, Alan Beecher and Jennifer Elliott for additional proofreading and comments, the Sussex Archaeological Society, the National Portrait Gallery, the *Bexhill Observer*, the East Sussex Record Office, the Hastings Area Archaeological Research Group and Bexhill Museum Association.

Particular mention must be made of L.J. Bartley, for his research and his book *The Story of Bexhill*.

I would also like to thank Emma, Kerri and Rachel for their support while writing this book.

One

THE BEGINNING

'Bexhill was a tiny village crowded in between the venerable church and ancient manor house, nestling among trees and looking down across breezy slopes on the white coastguard station and the open Channel. Between it and St Leonards there were scarce half-a-dozen houses, and the road still had its high hedges full of brambles and wild flowers all the way into the village; and a very pleasant looking old village it must have been.

'First, as one passed two great corn-stacks, which seem to have stood from time immemorial on the same spot, one saw across a little hollow the church and handsome rectory standing among the trees of the park-like glebe; then the road ran by a long, quaint house, which in process of time had grown by adaptation out of the stabling and offices of an old coal mine (or, rather, of a mine for coal, seeing that, notwithstanding £80,000 spent looking for it, no coal ever came to light), and past the gables of the old manor house, with its choked stew-pond below; and so, underneath the boughs of a huge

1　*Cottage by the beach, 1868. View of the bottom of Sea Lane from a nearby field.*

2   *Bexhill from the south-east, 1863. In the view from Galley Hill, Marine Cottages are on the left and St Peter's church is at the top of the hill. Part of Marine Cottages may originally have been a building associated with the 1806 coal-mining attempt.*

walnut tree, into the "street," to the ancient inn, and quaint old church with its dormer windows and stuccoed tower; or, turning to the left, past a quasi-modern house in which tradition says the "Iron Duke" once quartered, and by the village smithy, one reached the brow of a steep declivity, and saw, across some half-mile of corn and pasture, the wide bright blue of the Channel, with the broad sweep of Pevensey Bay and all the country up to Beachy Head girdling round the lowlands like a picture-frame.

'Here, if not on historic ground, we are at any rate within sight of it, and can well imagine that from here some terrified group of Britons or triumphant heathens watched the awful flames of smoking Anderida in the distance … Here, also, had been a fine post of observation for Harold's men when William landed at Pevensey.'[1]

This picturesque description of what is now Bexhill Old Town in the 1870s is from Dr Wills' book *Bexelei to Bexhill*, published in 1888. This walk around the village starts from the east, approaching by the now truncated Hastings Road leading up from Bulverhythe, the ancient route taken by the coastwise King's highway. Bexhill's once conspicuous hill-top village, manor house and church have been a focal point and centre of administration for centuries. Recorded as 'Bexhill Hill' in the Manor Court Rolls, it is named elsewhere as 'The Hill'.

Bexhill is situated on the coast of East Sussex between Pevensey on the west and Hastings to the east; inland to the north is Battle. Today Bexhill is not so well known as it deserves to be. This almost certainly would not have been the case one hundred years ago as the town was then an up-and-coming fashionable resort, whose civic leaders believed that they could compete with and out-do any other seaside venue in the south-east.

The parish of Bexhill roughly coincides with the later borough of Bexhill, an area of some eight thousand acres (3,237 hectares). The coastline runs from the boundary with Bulverhythe to the east along to the far side of Normans Bay. Bexhill includes the communities of Pebsham, Sidley, Cooden, Little Common, Barnhorn and Normans Bay, as well as the Old Town (the former Bexhill village and Belle Hill) and the town centre and seafront of the late Victorian resort, Bexhill-on-Sea. Topographically Bexhill resembles a triangle-shaped area of high ground with the valley of the Watermill Stream to the north, the Combe Haven valley to the east and the Pevensey Levels to the west. This geographic unit, with its

high level springs and stream, made the area largely self-contained and distinct from the surrounding countryside.

Starting with the very bones of Bexhill, the rocks on which it stands, the local geology is part of the Wealden formation composed of Wadhurst Clay, Ashdown Beds and Tunbridge Wells Sands. These are siltstones, sandstones and clays and are about 130 million years old. All these sedimentary rocks were deposited in a low-lying freshwater environment.

The best place to explore Bexhill's geology is on the beach, which yields a surprising range of fossils; track-ways of dinosaur footprints are often exposed at low water and fossilised dinosaur bone is sometimes found after winter storms. The majority of dinosaur remains are from Iguanodon, a five- to eight-metre long plant-eating animal that lived here, or at least passed through in large numbers during the

3   Bexhill seafront, 23 July 1868. South Cliff, the rock formation, is the side view of 'Bessie's Apron'.

Lower Cretaceous period. Less common are the bones and teeth of meat-eating dinosaurs, most of which are usually grouped together under the name of Megalosaurus but probably represent a range of different species. Rare finds include the occasional tooth of Baryonyx, a fish-eating dinosaur with hooked claws and a crocodile-like snout; a single tooth of a small, swift, meat-eating Velociraptor-like dinosaur; and a significant part of the skeleton of an armoured plant-eating dinosaur Polacanthus.

Associated with the dinosaur finds are fossils of the other plants and animals with which they co-existed: ferns, seed-ferns, conifers, molluscs, crustaceans, fish, sharks, turtles, crocodiles and lizards. Pieces of amber, the fossilised sap from coniferous trees, have also been found, but as yet no specimens with preserved insects.

Tree roots, trunks and branches are occasionally uncovered beneath the sand on the beach and perfectly preserved hazel nuts have been found washed up in rock pools. These finds are often confused with fossil wood and lignite on the beach but are from a much younger, although still ancient period. These waterlogged remains are from a submerged forest that runs along the coast.

The submerged forest was originally assumed to be due to the inundation caused by the storms of 1250 and 1287, events of almost biblical proportions that wrecked shipping all along the south coast, caused the river Rother to change its course and led to the abandonment of old Winchelsea. However, carbon-dating on some of the remains has shown them to be much older than this. They are in fact some four thousand years old, taking us back to the end of

4 *'Bessie's Apron', 5 August 1868. This was the remains of a stack at South Cliff. The rock formation was named after its shape, which the woman in this watercolour is demonstrating. Presumably there was once a top section making the outline look more like a woman wearing a hooped skirt and apron.*

5 *The beach at West Cliff: watercolour by M. Oliver, 1891. West Cliff is now known as South Cliff.*

the Neolithic or New Stone Age and the start of the Bronze Age.

We know very little about prehistoric settlement in the area but Bexhill Museum has a fine collection of stone tools found within the borough boundary, indicating much human activity. The oldest remains are microliths from the Mesolithic or Middle Stone Age, tiny flint blades that were fastened together to form composite tools. These date back some six to eight thousand years and are from a period before the development of farming in this country. The Mesolithic people of Bexhill would have been hunter-gatherers in a largely wooded landscape; finds have been discovered at Galley Hill and in the Old Town, high ground from where, perhaps, the movement of game was observed.

More numerous are flints from the Neolithic such as scrapers, arrowheads and axes. These people were the first farmers who probably cleared the surrounding woodland in order to create fields and keep cattle. The best evidence of later prehistoric activity is a hoard of Bronze-Age axe-heads found at Culver Croft Bank, in the western part of Bexhill. Two of these Middle Bronze-Age axes or palstaves are displayed in Bexhill Museum and are about three thousand years old.

In the Iron Age and early Roman period Bexhill seems to have been on the western border of the tribal area of the Cantiaci or Canti, after whom the county of Kent is named. The boundary between the Cantiaci and the Regni, who were to the west, is thought to have been through the Pevensey

6   *Mesolithic flint tools found in Bexhill.*

7   *Neolithic flint tools found in Bexhill. From left to right, a knife found at Galley Hill, a scraper found in the Old Town, a chisel re-cut from a broken polished axehead from Broadoak Park, and a late Neolithic barbed and tanged arrowhead, also from Broadoak Park.*

Levels. Even in the early historic period the area now occupied by Hastings and Rother District, of which Bexhill is the westernmost part, seems to have had a distinct identity from Sussex and Kent. The place-name of Hastings or Hæstingas or Hæstingorum was applied to this whole area, not just the present town of Hastings.[2]

One unusual find from a garden in Bexhill was a carved granite head. It is suggested that this may be of Romano-Celtic origin but there is no archaeological context and it cannot be accurately dated or proved to be of local origin. Roman pottery has been found on Hooe Level suggesting settlement here, which contradicts the idea that the Pevensey Levels was a tidal inlet at this time.

There are reports of the discovery of ancient boats in Bexhill: Charles Dawson described one in the *Sussex Archaeological Collections* of 1894 and another was reported when Egerton Park was created in 1888. Dawson is now suspected of being a prodigious hoaxer and has been linked with the famous 'Piltdown Man' hoax, so the 'Bexhill Boat' episode may be a matter of 19th-century social history rather than archaeology. There is no reason to doubt the Egerton Park find because this area corresponds with the position of a lagoon-like feature until it was excavated when the resort developed, although the boat could have dated from almost any period.

Within the bounds of Bexhill there were iron-working sites or bloomeries at Buckholt and Sidley, following the course of Watermill Stream. Some of these bloomeries may date back to the Roman

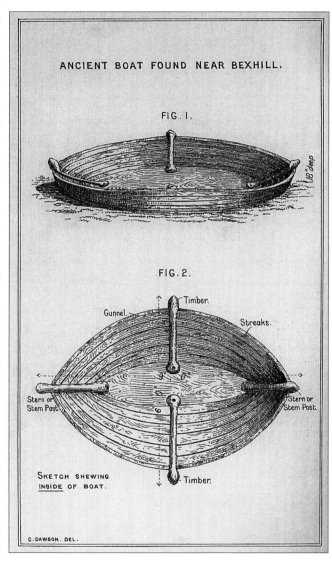

8 *Charles Dawson's ancient boat from Bexhill. (From* Sussex Archaeological Collections *1894. Reproduced by permission of the Sussex Archaeological Society.)*

9 *Terraces in Bexhill Hill. This image from the prospectus of the Church Farm Estate c.1937 provides the only known visual record of the terraces on the north side of the hill. They are also noted on the south side suggesting that they may have originally encircled the hill. The photograph is taken from Holliers Hill and shows St Peter's church on the skyline and Chantry Lane to the right.*

period and there is the possibility that they were based on earlier Iron-Age sites.[3] Just beyond Crowhurst on Bexhill's north-eastern border is a Roman iron-working site of gargantuan proportion, Beauport Park. It is famous for the bathhouse that was preserved by being buried under a landslide of iron slag. It has even been suggested that at its peak it was one of the main iron-producing sites in the entire Empire. The Roman navy, the Classis Britannica, ran the iron-works and it seems likely that the whole area including Bexhill was part of an industrial zone at this time.

Even at this comparatively late stage when we pass from the prehistoric into the historic period there is still little to suggest what settlement was like in the area we now know as Bexhill. It is probable that the land was farmed in one way or another from the Neolithic, with a dispersed pattern of settlement set amongst fields. Bexhill was to have an almost entirely agricultural economy until the end of the 19th century.

Two

LORDSHIP OF THE CHURCH

The place-name of Bexhill has had various spellings over the years from Bixlea or Bexlia, Bexelei, Bexle, Beksela, Beause to Buxle. These are based on two basic place-names, Bexley and Bexhill, each with variations in language and spelling. It is possible that the names are referring to different things, the district of Bexley and the settlement of Bexhill Hill within it. It has been suggested that Bexhill means 'windy hill', which is certainly appropriate, or 'Box tree clearing', or literally Beckeslea, perhaps referring to the many high level land springs and streams activated following heavy rain.

Place-name evidence is hard to interpret and the original meaning of Bexhill may now be lost. Locally there are place-names with 'ton' or 'ham' endings, such as Collington, Worsham and Pebsham, which suggest Saxon origins; Kayworth, 'kæia weorð' in the Offa charter, is a notable exception and may be derived from 'caer', a Celtic or Ancient British word.

10 *Bexhill from 'Sicklas' or Sickles pond, 1868. The double hedge line on the left is a farm track, leading to the Manor House from the south-east.*

Durham chroniclers noted that in AD 771 King Offa of Mercia (757-96) forcibly subjugated a people known as the Hæstingas. It has been suggested that the Hæstingas might have been Christian colonists who moved into the eastern edge of Sussex from Kent.[1] It is likely that the Hæstingas were of Kentish origin, but they probably moved to this area before adopting Christianity. A rewritten version of an AD 772 King Offa charter, copied into a 13th-century Canterbury church register, records his grant of land at Bexhill, named as 'Bexlea', to Bishop Oswald (Osa) of the emerging South-Saxon community at Selsey. The purpose was to build a monasterium, a minster or administrative church, an outpost of the distant Selsey basilica. This is believed to be the first written reference to Bexhill. A possible date for the re-writing is about 1148-50, when Bexhill was returned to church ownership. That there was a genuine eighth-century charter on which the 13th-century copy is based seems likely but some mistakes, or even alterations that might have benefited the bishops, may have occurred when it was transcribed.[2]

The 772 Charter is set out in Appendix 1, and is based on Eric Barker's translation.[3] When the charter was re-written it appears that certain lines were transposed by mistake, a process known as inversion; this version was researched and prepared for Bexhill Museum.

The land described in the charter is on the western side of Bexhill, in what is now Cooden and Barnhorn, in Ninfield Hundred rather than Bexhill Hundred. It clearly is not describing the area of the modern Bexhill old town, which raises some awkward questions. It is usually assumed that the church

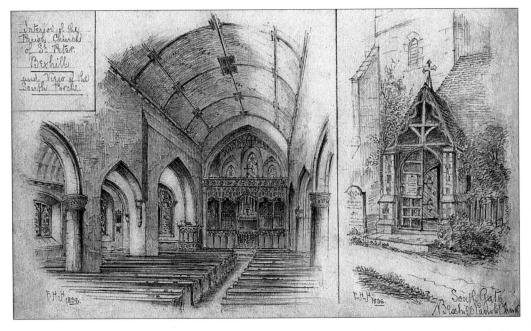

11 *Pencil drawing of the interior of the east end of St Peter's church and the exterior of the south porch, by F.H.H., 1896.*

12 *Watercolour of St Peter's church by M.D. Myatt, August 1851. This shows the building before the 1878 modifications. Houses in Church Street can be seen on the left.*

mentioned in the charter is St Peter's in Bexhill old town, but this area is not described in the charter.

When St Peter's church was altered in 1878 to Victorian taste, two important discoveries were made in the nave; firstly, it is recorded that 'herring-bone' stonework was discovered under the plaster suggesting Saxon origins, and, secondly, an intricately carved slab of stone was unearthed under the floor. The slab, known as the Bexhill Stone, is a fine example of Saxon stonework and may date from the eighth to early tenth century. It is believed to be the lid of a box that contained holy relics and as such would imbue the church with its spiritual authority; if it were an original fixture within the church it supports the idea that it was the minster church founded by King Offa.

The charter indicates that Bexhill was an important place before the Norman Conquest. The minster church would have been the focal place in the surrounding countryside. Mark Gardiner identifies the parochia of Bexhill including the churches of Ninfield, Hooe and, in Hastings, All Saints cum St Andrews, St Clements and Holy Trinity.[4]

Vikings raided the Sussex coast between 792 and 1011, but there is no record of how this affected Bexhill. However, the later events of 1066 did have an impact. William the Conqueror landed near Pevensey, established a fortification at Hastings and then moved north to fight King Harold's army at the site later named Battle. All the documentary evidence we have for the effect these events had on Bexhill comes from King William's Domesday Survey of 1086.

13 *The Bexhill Stone, perhaps the finest piece of carved Saxon stonework in Sussex. Dating from the 9th or early 10th century, this is probably the lid of a box containing holy relics. The Stone was discovered under the nave of St Peter's church when it was altered in 1878.*

In Bexhill Hundred: Osbern holds Bexhill from the Count [of Eu]. Before 1066 Bishop Alric held it because it is the bishopric's; he held it later until King William gave the castelry of Hastings to the Count. Before 1066 and now it answered for 20 hides. Land for 26 ploughs. The Count [of Eu] holds 3 hides of the land of this manor himself in lordship. He has 1 plough; 7 villagers with 4 ploughs. Osbern has 10 hides of this land; Venning 1 hide; William of Sept-Meules less ½ virgate; Robert St Leger 1 hide and ½ virgate; Reinbert ½ hide; Ansketel ½ hide; Robert of Criel ½ hide; the clerics Geoffrey and Roger 1 hide in prebend; 2 churches. In lordship 4 ploughs; 46 villagers and 27 cottagers with 29 ploughs. In the whole manor, meadow, 6 acres. Value of the whole manor before 1066 £20; later it was waste; now £18 10s; the Count's part 40s thereof.

Osbern holds 2 virgates of land from the Count [of Eu] in this Hundred. It always answered for 2 virgates. He has 5 oxen in a plough. The value was 8s; now 16s.[5]

So Bexhill was worth £20 before the Conquest, had no value after 1066 and by 1086 at £18 10s. it had still not recovered to its pre-invasion value.

There is also mention of two churches in Bexhill. One is certainly St Peter's church but it is not known where the second one was. It is possible that the other church may not be in modern Bexhill at all; it could have been a reference to Icklesham church. Entries in the Chichester Chartulary refer to the restitution of 'Bixla with its churches and hundred, Ichelesham and Wikham'.[6] Architecturally there are many similarities between Bexhill's parish church and that of Icklesham, and it has been suggested that the same craftsmen may have worked on them. A Norman tower was added to St Peter's after the invasion.

Sussex was divided into five units called rapes, and was the only county subdivided in this way. King William put a Norman baron in charge of each rape; they established castles transforming the rapes into castleries. Within each rape were smaller areas of land called hundreds and each hundred was made up of manors. The manors mentioned in Domesday Book do not necessarily relate to the later medieval manors. Bexhill Manor was within Bexhill Hundred in the Rape of Hastings. The Rape of Hastings strongly resembled the ancient Hæstingas or Hæstingorum, the tribal area of the people of Hastings. Barnhorn and parts of Cooden, although within the parish of Bexhill, were part of Ninfield Hundred. The parish of Bexhill and the manor of Bexhill are not the same and, while mostly overlapping, they described different areas of land, one church-based the other secular.

The invasion introduced the feudal system to England. The Norman barons in William's army were rewarded for their support with grants of land, and so replaced much of the Anglo-Saxon aristocracy. Knights supported the barons and were awarded knights fees, land they held from the barons in return for military service. The bishops of Selsey had owned Bexhill manor but William gave it to Robert Count of Eu, along with the rest of the Rape of Hastings. Bexhill was annexed to the collegiate church of St Mary, established within Hastings Castle, so ecclesiastical power shifted, post-Conquest, from Bexhill to Hastings.[7]

Another local repercussion of the 1066 invasion was the establishment of an abbey near the site of the battlefield where King Harold was defeated. Battle Abbey was a powerful symbol of Norman supremacy; it was to cast a long shadow across the later history of Bexhill. The abbey claimed the right to appeal directly to the king rather than through the established church hierarchy, which set it at odds with the bishops of Selsey who held Bexhill.

There was some question over the legitimacy of Eu's possession of Bexhill and the bishops wanted it back. The seat of the diocese was moved from Selsey to Chichester in 1075, the bishops of Selsey becoming the bishops of Chichester. At Rheims in April 1148 Bishop Hilary received the support of Pope Eugenius III in his attempt to recover the diocese's lost possessions.[8] Robert's grandson John, Count of Eu, announced that he was to give Bexhill back to the bishops in 1148; the transfer was processed in 1149 and finalised in 1150. The bishops replaced the Counts of

14 *Church Street, Bexhill Village, by F.H.H., 1896. The churchyard is on the left.*

15 *Church Street, c.1920. The walnut was cut down in 1906 but the ivy-covered stump was not removed until 1921. The building next to the church lych-gates was originally a Wealden hall house.*

Eu as Bexhill's feudal lord, holding Bexhill directly of the king. Their ownership of Bexhill was as a secular lord and quite separate from their ecclesiastical authority over the diocese. Bexhill had returned to the bishops of Chichester, who held onto it until the middle of the 16th century.

A number of documents held by the Chartulary of Chichester concern the restoration of Bexhill to the bishops of Chichester in 1148-50. One of the later documents mentions a court of arbitration attended by Theobald, Archbishop of Canterbury (named as Papal Legate), the Bishop of Lincoln and Sir William of Ypres; they awarded knights fees in Bexhill to Bishop Hilary of Chichester. The presence of the archbishop suggests that the court was held in Canterbury, where at this time Stephen's Queen Matilda was resident and Sir William of Ypres was her military commander. The restoration of Bexhill must be seen in the context of the anarchy caused by the struggle between King Stephen and Empress Matilda. Canterbury was the base of the forces opposed to Empress Matilda. Empress Matilda and Queen Matilda were

LORDSHIP OF THE CHURCH

cousins and both descendants of the Anglo-Saxon kings.

In 1141 Empress Matilda had held King Stephen captive but Stephen's Queen Matilda, through Sir William of Ypres, had captured the Empress' main military supporter, the Duke of Gloucester. The Empress could not successfully pursue her claim to the throne without the Duke of Gloucester's help, so an exchange of prisoners was negotiated and they were released. Shortly afterwards the Duke of Gloucester died. Unable to continue without him, Empress Matilda gave up and returned to France.

King Stephen ultimately won the civil conflict in England but lost the one in Normandy. It must be remembered that Sussex was strategically important as the main transport route between the two countries.

The church had originally accepted Empress Matilda and was not on good terms with King Stephen, who had exiled the Archbishop of Canterbury and refused to appoint the bishop of York because his favoured candidate, Bishop Hilary, was rejected by Rome. Queen Matilda with the help of William of Ypres, the Archbishop of Canterbury and Bishop Hilary managed to reconcile King Stephen with the church. Restoration of lost lands, including Bexhill, was almost certainly part of Hilary's reward for his support.

During the reign of King Stephen hostility grew between Bishop Hilary of Chichester and Abbot Walter de Luci of Battle as the abbot refused to obey the bishop. This culminated in a royal hearing of 1157 when King Henry II upheld the abbey's claim of immunity from the bishop's jurisdiction. This was as much a political struggle as it was a religious one. The abbot's brother Richard de

16 *Cooden Moat, 1894. Douglas Young, son of Henry Young of Cooden Mount, is shown climbing the tree.*

Luci held high office in both King Stephen's and King Henry II's reigns. Much of what is known comes from 'The Chronicle of Battle Abbey'. Although this does not directly mention Bexhill's role in the feud, Battle Abbey would have wished to expand south and secure property on the coast, both for economic reasons and for the prestige it would bring. It was in the interests of the Crown to keep on good terms with the lords of the Sussex coast, as their support was necessary in defending the country from invasion.

15

17 *Pencil drawing of a house at Worsham, 1873.*

Much of Cooden or Cowden belonged to the Coding family, the earliest recorded member being William de Coding in 1242. In 1304 John de Coding resolved a dispute that he had with the abbot of Battle concerning grazing rights at Coding-dune. A moated site, possibly for a manor house, still survives at Cooden and may be associated with the de Coding family, signifying their local importance in the 13th and 14th centuries. Tenancy passed to the Brenchley family at the end of 14th century and by 1411 Joan Brenchley held the manor. Lordship of Cooden Manor passed from the Rape of Hastings to St Stephen's College, Westminster. The lordship finally passed to the Sackville family, who also owned the manor of Bexhill and thus brought the two manors together.

The Domesday Survey shows that Bexhill Hundred contained the manor of Bullington, which included the land later known as Pebsham. Tréport Abbey is recorded as in possession of much of Bullington, while the Count of Eu held the remainder. The abbey sold the holding to the Cistercian abbey at Robertsbridge in 1196, payment for this exchange not being completed until 1290. The monks at Battle would perhaps not have welcomed the presence of a different monastic order so close by, holding land that they themselves would have wanted. Pebsham was eventually returned to Bexhill, but Bullington, including Bulverhythe, became part of Hastings as a non-corporate member of the Cinque Ports.

The first known tenant of Pebsham was John de Peplesham, who held the manor from Tréport in 1254. Simon de Peplesham held it by 1348. His granddaughter Joan Batisford married Sir William Brenchley, and later founded a chantry at her husband's tomb in Canterbury. In her will of 1453 she also left instructions for a chantry chapel in Bexhill's parish church, known as the Batisford Chapel. In 1364 the manor of Buckholt was granted to William Batisford and in 1412 Joan Brenchley held it. Iron-working later developed in Buckholt and by 1574 Lord Dacre held a forge and a furnace there.

About 1138 the monks of Battle had been evicted from a Barnhorn estate that they claimed had been obtained by a gift and purchase from Withelard de Baillol (Bailleul) and his vassal Ingleran called 'Beccheneridere' or 'beacon-rider'. Ingleran was an ancestor of the 'de Northeye' family who also owned the Buckholt estate; the name 'ridere' implies Anglo-Saxon descent. The monks had spent money building a mill and improving their acquisition at Barnhorn and refused to pay further charges. About 1160 Abbott Walter de Luci successfully protested to King Henry II, who ordered that the monks' estate be returned.

It is likely that, during the negotiated restoration of Bexhill to Bishop Hilary, the monks of Battle would have begun to agitate for reinstatement at Barnhorn. The long description of Barnhorn in the re-written Offa Charter is probably due to the bishop's need to establish ownership in the 12th century to prevent Battle Abbey attempting to claim the land.

In 1538 King Henry VIII granted Battle Abbey, including land at Barnhorn, to Sir Anthony Browne, whose son became Viscount Montague. Anthony, the 6th

Viscount, sold the Battle estates, including the manor of Barnhorn, to Sir Thomas Webster Bt. in 1721. The Webster finances soon began to deteriorate. In 1857 Sir Augustus Webster sold the heavily mortgaged Battle Abbey and its estates, including the land at Barnhorn, to Lord Harry Vane, who later became Duke of Cleveland. In 1861 the Duke also acquired the Barnhorn Hill estate. The Collins family had been owners of the Constable lands and had amalgamated a number of Barnhorn properties late in 1807 and in 1808. This is the reason that there are two 'Barnhorn Manor' house names in Barnhorn Road.

The eldest son of Sir Augustus Webster, also Augustus, married wealthy heiress Mabel Crossley in 1895. Mabel was the granddaughter of Joseph Crossley, the successful Yorkshire carpet manufacturer. Sir Augustus was thus able, in 1901, to repurchase Battle Abbey and its lands, including the two Barnhorn estates. The Barnhorn properties were subsequently sold.

John Fuller MP, popularly known as 'Mad Jack', is best known for building follies around Brightling. In 1810 his maternal uncle, John Fuller of Parkgate Catsfield, died, leaving John, his nephew and namesake, in possession of many Bexhill estates, including the Lunsford farmlands and the manor of Buckholt. John Fuller of Brightling died in 1834 and ownership of his Bexhill properties passed to a nephew, Sir Peregrine Palmer Fuller Acland Bt. Sir Peregrine obtained permission from Chancery to sell the estates. Earl Brassey bought the manor of Buckholt including land at Buckholt and Southeye (Rockhouse Bank). A stretch of coastal roadway at Norman's Bay, sold to the Commissioners of Sewers, was known as Brassey's Road.

The manor of Northey (Northeye) took its name from the most northerly of a cluster of marshland 'high fields' or 'eyes' located to the far west of Bexhill parish. It was later known as 'Chapel Field'. Mounds of desalinated soil, the remains of salt recovery, suggest that the area was originally bordered at times on the west and north by an inflow of tidal salt water.

The old droveway or treadway which links Chapel Field with Barnhorn was known until the early 18th century as 'the Trade', a name that derives from 'trada', a Saxon word for track. A legal agreement of 1248 refers to 'the pasture called the Trade' as a possession of William de Northeye, but the abbot of Battle had a right of way with livestock, providing they were not allowed to graze. As the droveway approaches Chapel Field there is a bridge and a confluence of footpaths, which is possibly the 'five ways' mentioned in the Offa Charter.

Following the Norman Conquest the tithes of 'Nordie' had been awarded to the Abbey of St Amand at Rouen. In the late 12th century Bishop Seffrid II of Chichester recovered the tithes for Bexhill parish from the abbess. In 1229 Northeye is listed as a limb of the Cinque Ports and it is through this connection that Bexhill's coat-of-arms includes a demi-hulk, the emblem of the Cinque Ports. The area around Northeye was known as the Liberty of the Sluice and was owned by the corporation of Hastings. Northeye's status as a limb of the Cinque Ports suggests a maritime role but this could have

18 *Chapel Field 1938. The site of the deserted medieval settlement of Northeye. Shown here during the excavation of the chapel site by Normandale School, the site is the pale patch in the upper middle section of the image. Chapel bridge is on the right-hand side.*

19 *Henry Sargent, on the left, showing the mayor of Bexhill, Gilbert Harry Goodwin, in the middle, the Bexhill Museum Association's excavation of Chapel Field, Northeye, 1952.*

been ship service and does not necessarily indicate that it was a port.

There is a deed of endowment for a chapel of St James at Northeye by William de Northeye in 1262; he was a descendant of Ingleran called 'Beccheneridere'. William is thought to have sided with the barons against King Henry III at the 1264 Battle of Lewes and so his estates were forfeited and provision made for his widow. The last reference to a chaplain at Northeye is in 1515. John Norden's map of 1595 shows the chapel, which is also mentioned in the 1656 addition to the 1650 Parliamentary survey. Budgen's county map of 1724 shows only a ruin, which seems to be incorrectly sited. The nature and extent of Northeye's settlement is uncertain. Councillor Ross of Hastings investigated the site in about 1850-7 and proposed that an earlier settlement of Northeye existed at Barnhorn and later moved to Chapel Field, which is incorrect. The chapel site was

excavated by Normandale School in 1938 and again by the Bexhill Museum Association in 1952; the first excavation was unfinished due to the start of the Second World War and the Museum's excavation was abandoned following an outbreak of foot-and-mouth disease on the marsh. The finds that survive from the second excavation are displayed within Bexhill Museum.

The marsh around Northeye was the site of many of the disputes between the bishops of Chichester and the abbots of Battle, being important both economically and strategically. It was valuable pasturage: stock could feed on the ample supply of vegetation on the wetlands and retreat to one of the scattered areas of high ground when the marsh flooded. Wallers Haven joined the sea at The Sluice, allowing the transport of cargo, that of wealden iron being particularly important. When Bishop Hilary recovered Bexhill in 1150 he also obtained the chaplaincy of Pevensey and so

20 *Court Lodge, 1872, Bexhill Manor House. 'Mrs B.' is written under the woman, presumably referring to Mrs Brook, wife of 'Squire' Arthur Sawyer Brook, who lived there at this time.*

had interests on both sides of the marsh; the establishment of Northeye Chapel in 1262 may have been an attempt by the bishops to consolidate their holdings and block the abbots' access to the coast.

When Bexhill's second oldest building, the manor house, was demolished in 1968, remains were discovered suggesting that parts of the building were 13th- or 14th-century. A possible date for the initial building of the manor house has been proposed at around 1250, when St Richard was bishop of Chichester. It was the easternmost residence of the bishops and they, or their representatives, would have stayed there when travelling around the diocese. Given the territorial disputes between the bishops of Chichester and the abbots of Battle, the episcopal visits to Bexhill and the manor house were probably occasions when they checked on their property.

In 1448 Adam de Moleyns, Bishop of Chichester, was granted a licence to 'empark 2,000 acres at Bexhill and to enclose and embattle his manor of the said name'. It is not known if this work was ever undertaken and Adam's death in 1450 may have ended the project. For most of its existence the manor house was referred to as Court Lodge, because it was where the manor court was held. The building was the administrative centre for Bexhill and was located close to the religious centre, St Peter's church.

Three

LORDSHIP OF THE
SACKVILLE FAMILY

Henry VIII sold Battle Abbey in 1538 during the Dissolution of the Monasteries. This event removed the bishop of Chichester's old rivals; the bishop's Bexhill holdings were also valued at this time, but no action was taken against them. More important to Bexhill than the Dissolution of the Monasteries was the suppression of chantries, colleges and free chapels that began under Henry VIII, and gathered strength under Edward VI. In particular, a December 1547 Act of Parliament under the boy-king Edward VI closed the Batisford Chantry in St Peter's church, took Chantry Farm and the farm of Northeye chapel out of church hands, and removed Cooden Manor from the possession of St Stephen's College, Westminster.

The bishop's local influence did not long outlast the abbot's. The Act of Exchange of 1559 gave Queen Elizabeth I the power to seize the land of vacant bishoprics and in 1561 the bishopric of Chichester fell vacant. Elizabeth did not reappoint and the land passed to the Crown. The queen granted Bexhill manor to

21 *Bexhill church and village 1888: watercolour by Annie Becken (1869-1935). The view is from the south-east, showing the houses in Church Street on the left and the rectory on the right.*

her friend, relative and supporter Sir Thomas Sackville, Lord Buckhurst; his descendants were the Earls and later Dukes of Dorset. The Sackvilles already had an interest in this area, Richard Sackville, Thomas' father, having acquired farmland at Cooden and Northeye before 1570.

Bexhill was no longer under church control and its future lay in secular hands. From a practical point of view life in Bexhill was not greatly changed and the resident farmers simply changed from one landowner to a new one. The bishops had never been permanently resident in Bexhill and this was true of their successors; both had much grander residences elsewhere and only business or, indeed, pleasure had brought them down for occasional short stays.

During Elizabeth's reign England was once more threatened with invasion. In 1587 coastal defences were erected around the Cooden Stream and fire-beacons were set up on Cooden Down to give warning of the approach of the Spanish Armada.

In 1597 Dr Pye, the rector of St Peter's church, established Bexhill's first school in the Batisford Chapel. Schools were to become a vital part of the town's economy during the late 19th century and throughout most of the twentieth.

Bexhill seems to have been in the enviable position of passing peacefully through the Civil War period. Manor court records are lacking. In 1650 the Parliamentarians began to record 'the possessions of Charles Stewart[*sic*], late King of England'. Their reports included

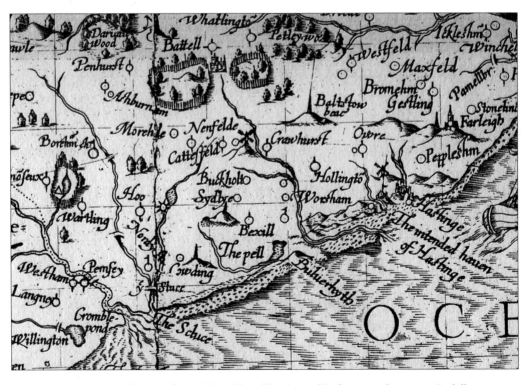

22 *John Norden map of 1595. Note 'The pell', a lagoon-like feature on the coast at Bexhill.*

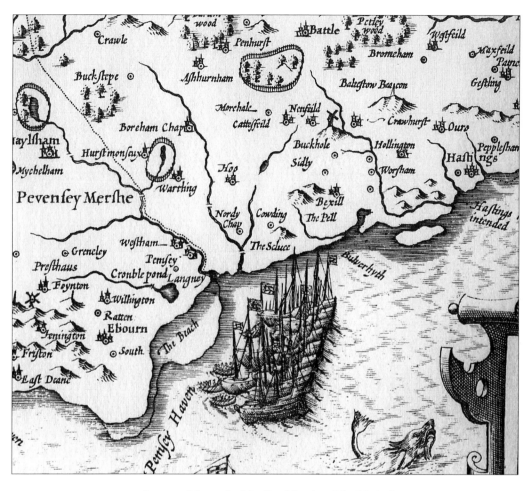

23   *1610 map of Sussex by John Speed based on John Norden's map.*

two parts of Bexhill: lands in Bexhill, Hooe and Barnhorn that had once belonged to the chaplain of Northeye, and lands of the Manor of Pevensey within the parish of Bexhill.

The Earls of Dorset, who were always close to the monarchy, were out of favour with the Parliamentarians during the Interregnum and lost much of their wealth and influence. Following the restoration of King Charles II, and increasing prosperity, successful merchants began to acquire and assemble large estates.

Bexhill had its first lady of the manor in 1677, Frances, Countess of Dorset. She was the daughter and heiress of Lionel Cranfield, Earl of Middlesex, and she had married Richard Sackville, the 4th Earl of Dorset. She inherited the manor when her husband died; she was later remarried to Henry Powle, Master of the Rolls, in 1679. The court records do not mention a lord or lady of the manor again until 1688 when her son Richard Sackville acquired the title.

24 *A portion of Richard Budgen's map of 1724 showing Bexhill.*

The 18th century was punctuated by some dramatic local events. A pamphlet written by Richard Budgen for the Royal Society recorded 'The Passage of the Hurricane from the Sea Side at Bexhill in Sussex to Newingden-Level, the twentieth day of May, 1729'. This describes a very severe but localised tornado-like storm that cut a swathe of destruction across Bexhill Down, Sidley and Buckholt before moving inland. A feature of some early maps of Sussex is a river ending in a lagoon-like feature at Bexhill referred to as The Pell, perhaps meaning pool.

In 1748 the Dutch East Indiaman *Amsterdam* was wrecked off Bulverhythe, its remains being periodically looted by the poor of Bexhill parish. Soldiers of the Bexhill-based King's German Legion attempted to recover the cargo of the *Amsterdam* in 1810, but they did not succeed.

Bexhill's parish register had been started in 1558. During the 18th century there was an increase in Bexhill's population and many of the local surnames still familiar in the area first appear in the parish register. Other entries record unknown persons found drowned on the shore. An entry dated 1776 records payments to William Curtis for the treatment of Sarah Davis for leprosy. It states that if she was not cured within two years he would get no further payment. As the matter is not mentioned again it appears that he was unsuccessful.

Architecturally, most of Bexhill Old Town's buildings date back to the 18th century, although many are hidden behind late Victorian weatherboarding. The first mention of the *Bell Hotel* is in 1751, although the building itself may have been a 17th-century residence. The *Bell* has always been an important part of Bexhill village; its Assembly Room was added in the 18th century to serve as a theatre for travelling players and a meeting place for the community. During the coaching era of the 18th and early 19th centuries it was a staging post; passengers would be picked up from the *Bell* and taken to Ninfield where they could catch the Brighton to Hastings coaches. Bexhill was at the axis of the coast road from Hastings to Eastbourne and the inland route through Sidley to Horsebridge, near Hailsham,

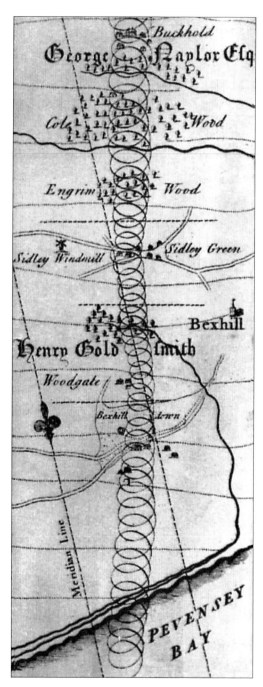

25 *Richard Budgen's map of 1729 showing the passage of a 'hurricane'.*

26 *High Street, Bexhill village: an oil painting by Charles Graves, dated 1899. On the right is the Reeves' grocers shop and in the distance is the gate to Barrack Hall.*

27 *The Bell Inn, August 1866, the social centre of Bexhill village since the 18th century. This watercolour shows the Bell before the new façade was added in 1888.*

28 *The Bell Hotel, c.1928, clearly showing the 1888 façade.*

and then Lewes. By the early 19th century the stagecoaches ran directly through Bexhill. The *Bell* was substantially modified in 1888 when it gained its present façade. The *New Inn* in Sidley and the *Wheatsheaf* in Little Common also probably date to the 18th century and served a similar function in their communities. The *Wheatsheaf* was expanded and altered in 1886.

The parish workhouse was built in 1755 on Bexhill Down, on the present site of King Offa School. The Battle workhouse replaced this when the local Poor Law Union was formed in 1834; the Bexhill site was afterwards called Workhouse Field. Bexhill was one of the fourteen parishes which made up the Battle Union, and did not begin to regain its independence until it grew as a resort and formed its Local Board of Health in 1884.

In 1760 Horace Walpole wrote to his friend George Montague Esq, 'I have found … that in the church of Beckley or Bexley in Sussex there are portraits of Henry III and his Queen.'[1] He asks his friend to find out more, as he wanted to use an illustration of the stained glass as the frontispiece of his book *Anecdotes of Painting*. Walpole acquired the window by 1771 and installed it in the chapel of his home at Strawberry Hill. The window was eventually returned to Bexhill and the portraits are thought to represent Christ and the Blessed Virgin Mary.

29 *The Salt Box, Church Street, 13 August 1866.*

The *Morning Post and Daily Advertiser* of Friday 28 January 1780 recorded that there was a witch trial at Bexhill, a surprisingly late date for an event of this kind and not taken particularly seriously by the reporter. It was claimed that two women of 'Beck's Hill' were accused of witchcraft and ostracised by the community. The women, who were almost starving, went to the parson at Hastings, as no one in Bexhill would help them. According to the report the parson referred then to a lawyer and he to the mayor of Hastings. All of them assembled and resolved the situation by weighing each of the women against the church's Bible. When the women were found to be heavier than the bible they were declared innocent of the charge of witchcraft, given a certificate to prove this, and reintegrated into the parish of Bexhill.

Four

COAL MINING, SOLDIERS AND SMUGGLERS

The end of the 18th century and the start of the 19th were dominated by war with France. Bexhill began to be militarised when a militia camp was established on Bexhill Common in 1794 and later barracks were built on Belle Hill in 1798. These were the lower barracks, later referred to as 'the Old Barracks'. More barracks were built further up Belle Hill when Bexhill became a base for soldiers of the Hanoverian King's German Legion, between 1804 and 1814. Napoleon had assembled an invasion force across the Channel in 1804 and, to defend against it, Martello Towers supported by barracks were planned all along the south-east coast. The invasion threat had passed by the time work began on the Martello Towers, but they were built as a deterrent against any future threat.

When construction of the Towers and additional barracks began in late 1804 and

30 *Army camp on Bexhill Common, 1794. Pevensey Bay is seen here before the construction of the Martello Towers. The building at the bottom right is the workhouse on Bexhill Down.*

31 *Martello Towers along Pevensey Bay viewed from Little Common, c.1820.*

1805, new wells were sunk to provide water. During this work black lignite or fossil wood was discovered, both on the coast and inland; it was thought to be coal, and the existence of a strata of this badly needed commodity was postulated. Those used to beachcombing in Bexhill will be familiar with the fragments of carbonised wood to be seen in the bedrock. These coal-like remains led to an expensive mistake.

In 1805 Arabella Diana, Duchess Dowager of Dorset, commissioned William James (1771–1837), colliery owner, land-agent, surveyor and promoter, to report on the mineralogy of the Sackville estates in Bexhill. Arabella was at that time controlling the estate on behalf of her infant son George John Frederick, Duke of Dorset. James was encouraged by his findings and recommended the formation of

a company to prospect for coal, stating that he would take a stake in that company. The Sussex Mining Company was created and William James became treasurer and chief investigator. He was also appointed Steward of the Manor of Bexhill. One of the main enthusiasts for the project was Josias Routledge, who in 1793 had bought 'Rosiers', a large house at the top of Bexhill Hill, with the adjoining land. He also built 'Millfield' on the upper part of Belle Hill around 1809-10.

In June 1806 the *Sussex Weekly Advertiser* reported that 'a vein of exceedingly fine coal' had been discovered in Bexhill. The search for coal had begun in a small enclosure near the sea, apparently not far from the present-day De La Warr Parade. A pit 27 feet deep had been sunk, followed by boring to a total depth of 164 feet. Here a 3ft. 6in. thick stratum

32   *Bexhill village and Holliers Hill, c.1860-70. Pencil drawing from Haddocks Hill, from the north-north-west. Belle Hill is on the right.*

33   *Millfield, Belle Hill: oil painting by Charles Graves dated 1904. Josias Routledge built Millfield in c.1809-10 and from 1843 to 1898 it was the home of Samuel Scrivens, who was second only to Earl De La Warr among the main landowners in Bexhill and developed London Road that was on his property.*

was mistakenly identified as 'strong coal'. The Sussex Mining Company soon began to sink a shaft on the site and then another on Bexhill Down. The shafts (or pits) continually flooded and had to be pumped out. Two 'fire' (steam) engines were installed and put to work, apparently with little success. In February 1807 the geologist John Farey had inspected the works at Bexhill and written that, in his opinion, it was impossible that coal would be found. In 1809, with nothing to show for their efforts, steam engines worn out and expenses mounting, some of the partners had become nervous and were allowed to quit the company. Exploration slowed. Digging continued until the start of 1810 when the works closed. James went on to promote other grand schemes and worked with Robert Stephenson on the Liverpool and Manchester Railway; he became bankrupt in 1823 and died impoverished in 1837. Josias Routledge, a partner in the coal-mining venture, was forced to mortgage and then sell his Bexhill properties. He was last reported living in Dieppe in 1822. William Thorpe of Hastings sold Millfield to Margaret Farrence in 1823. At least £30,000 had been invested in the scheme, not the £80,000 mentioned by Dr Wills in *Bexelei to Bexhill*, but no coal was ever found. The Bexhill coal-mining misadventure is significant because it allowed John Farey to demonstrate that if William Smith's new theory of stratification were appreciated expensive mistakes could be avoided in future.[1]

The archives of the Crown Estates contain a series of investigative documents that concern an elongated and unsuccessful mission to recover 'An estate called Northey', thought to have been the rightful property of the Crown. The series begins with an 1808 report made by surveyor A.E. Driver who, as part of his surreptitious enquiries, investigated the Belle Hill lands of a John Ockenden. Belle Hill was

34 *Farm house near Bexhill, 28 August 1863: Marine Cottages with Galley Hill are in the background. The long building with three chimneys behind the farmhouse is believed to be a structure associated with the coal-mining attempt of 1806.*

35 *The junction of Belle Hill and London Road, by Charles Graves, dated 1901. On the left is Pilbeam's butchers shop and further up on the right is Warburton's corn merchants and grain mill.*

at that time known as 'Belly Hill', a corrupted version of 'Bury Hill', a name recorded in the 18th-century manor court roll. Driver noted, 'At one part of the garden was a smaller and more recently built house occupied by his sister (in law) Lucy Ockenden'; also 'there are persons living who can remember when the house belonging to John Ockenden (senior) stood quite by itself, this bounded on all sides by an estate belonging to the same proprietor Mr Russell.' John Ockenden (junior), the eldest son, informed Driver that his father had purchased the estate about 55 years earlier. John Ockenden (senior) and his wife Elizabeth were married in 1756, an event which was celebrated by their descendants at a service in St Peter's church on 'Ockenden Day', 25 March 1991.

The King's German Legion soldiers would have been highly visible as they greatly out-numbered the local inhabitants from 1804 to 1814. Some five or six thousand Hanoverian soldiers arrived in a village that previously had a total population of about two thousand people.[2] They came to England following the French invasion of Hanover in 1803. The Elector of Hanover, being also King George III of Brit-ain, agreed to the men becoming part of the British Army but staying together as a German component, with George III's son, Adolphus Frederick, Duke of Cambridge, as their Colo-nel-in-Chief. King's German Legion officers who distinguished themselves at the Battle of Waterloo included Lieutenant-General Charles Count von Alten, Major-General Sir Colin Halkett, Lieutenant-Colonel Baron Christian

36 *The middle of Belle Hill, a pen and ink drawing by Charles Graves dated 1897. Amherst Road later joined Belle Hill here in 1898; the two houses on the left, roughly where the horse and cart is standing, were demolished when the road was built. An almost identical photograph exists, suggesting that Graves worked from this. At the end of the road Belle Hill continues on the right and the junction with Barrack Road is on the left. The building at the end of the road is Sycamore Cottage.*

von Ompteda, Colonel Hugh Halkett and Major George Baring. Von Alten was the only German officer ever to command a British Army Division. Ompteda wrote a diary, which includes his experiences in Bexhill, describing the difficult conditions at the barracks during his first autumn there in 1804. It was then still a tented camp and the turf huts were not completed until the winter. He fell ill and stayed with the Lansdell family at Woodsgate Farm to recuperate.

Bexhill served as the King's German Legion's main Infantry and Artillery Depots, while the cavalry was based at Weymouth with subsidiary depots at Ipswich, Guildford and Canterbury. The Bexhill barracks

was very extensive and dwarfed the actual village. The development of the settlement on Belle Hill seems to have been a response to the barracks' presence; traders set up shop outside the barrack gates, eager to supply a new market. The inns, the *Black Horse*, later renamed the *Queen's Head*, on Belle Hill, and the *Gun* on Bexhill Down may have opened due to the presence of the barracks. The *Gun* was run by Samuel Ockenden, brother of the John Ockenden interviewed in Driver's 1808 Survey. It is said that soldiers of the King's German Legion created a bowling alley at the *New Inn* at Sidley.

Although Bexhill was the base of the infantry, the troops were deployed in various campaigns in Europe. Bexhill was also home to their families, many of whom would have remained here while the soldiers were away. They had their own German school for their children, records of which are preserved in the Hanover Archive. Towards the end of the war burials in Bexhill record the death of older German men, possibly veterans based at the barracks. The Legion became part of the parish community and, as Ompteda wrote, 'The gentry round called at the camp. They seem to be beginning to discover that we are not quite outlandish bears.' Arthur Sawyer Brook recalled that one of his earliest memories was of the harmonious singing of the German soldiers in St Peter's church.

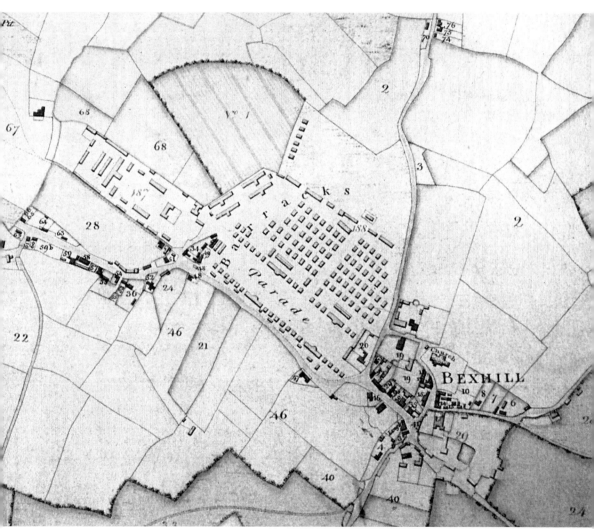

37 *A portion of the Duke of Dorset's 1808 survey map of Bexhill. The 'engine pit' at the top left is part of the 1806 coal-mining venture. The barracks, that were the base of the King's German Legion, dominate the village.*

38 *Pencil drawing of St Peter's church and the rectory from the north-east, c.1865. It is thought to be by Arthur John Brook.*

39 *Looking up Belle Hill: a pen and ink drawing by Charles Graves made in 1897. The building at the top of the hill on the left is the home of Henry Parker, the builder and undertaker. At the top of the hill Barrack Road goes off to the left and Belle Hill continues on the right. In the distance there are two structures. On the left in Barrack Road is a large building, the western end of the barrack's parade ground which was used by the Wilson Memorial School and later the National School; it has been suggested that the building was once part of the barracks but this has not been proved. On the right is Sycamore Cottage.*

40   *Belle Hill, at the junction of Amherst and Barrack Road: a pen and ink drawing by Charles Graves dated 1897, showing 59 Belle Hill, the home of Henry Parker, the builder and undertaker, with the adjoining workshop on the right. The business was founded in 1800 and from 1875 Frederick Parker also had a builder and undertaker's workshop at 22 Belle Hill. The view is from further up Belle Hill, the junction with Barrack Road is on the right, and the junction with Amherst Road and the lower part of Belle Hill on the left.*

Parts of the Legion served in the Peninsular War from 1809 and lost many men during the fighting. New soldiers were recruited who were not always German. These recruits were of several nationalities and included prisoners-of-war. It was also an opportunity for less well-off Englishmen who aspired to be officers to gain a commission in the Army.

Letters preserved at Bexhill Museum record a paternity suit of February 1813, between Sophia Brazier, the teenage daughter of the innkeeper of the *Black Horse* on Belle Hill, and Frederick Rehwinkell, an officer of the King's German Legion. The parish register reveals a steep increase in baptisms, marriages and burials at this time. Girls with local surnames married men with German ones; there are also brides and grooms both with German names. The ten-year period in which the King's German Legion was based in Bexhill undoubtedly enriched the genetic diversity of the community.

The Legion was withdrawn from Bexhill in 1814. It played a vital role in the Battle of Waterloo on 18 June 1815 by holding the strategically important farmhouse of La Haye Sainte, near the centre of the battlefield. During the battle the Legion suffered heavy casualties but, with Napoleon's defeat, Hanover was liberated and the survivors were able to return home. Little is known of the fate of the Bexhill girls who married German soldiers. Many would have been widowed in 1815 but presumably some went to start new lives with their husbands in the Hanover region.

After the King's German Legion had departed the barracks closed; buildings began to be removed from 1815 and the site was sold in 1822. Later, the settlement that had developed at the entrance to the barracks became known as 'Belle Hill' rather than 'Belly Hill'. The barracks had formed a link between the communities of Belle Hill and Bexhill village. Without it Belle Hill was left as a separate settlement, and it was not until the town grew in the 20th century that the two were re-connected. The Belle Hill Wesleyan chapel was built in 1825 on land previously part of the barracks site. It was used as a Methodist chapel until 1938 and the building is still standing.

Henry Dorling, stepfather of the famous Mrs Beeton, was a printer in Bexhill and it is recorded that he had the habit of praying in German – a side-effect of attending the school set up by the King's German Legion. The period saw the start of Bexhill's association with Germany that even two World Wars could not fully erase.

Dr Wills noted the local legend that the 'Iron Duke' of Wellington stayed in Bexhill; this is a possibility, if not established fact, as the Duke briefly commanded the forces at Hastings. Another unsubstantiated local legend, this one not quite so patriotic, is that Napoleon obtained his English newspapers from Bexhill smugglers. This dubious claim to fame is cited in passing by a 19th-century antiquarian who did not reveal his sources.

There is a mysterious mound in a field on the west side of Upper Sea Road, now part of the playing fields of St Peter and St Paul's School. The earthwork does not appear on the Duke of Dorset's 1808 map but is shown on the 1873 Ordnance Survey one, suggesting that it was created between these dates. Possible explanations include a windmill mound, a prospect mound for a formal garden, or an observation post associated with the barracks.

Smuggling was rife between 1700 and 1850 when high levels of taxation to fund foreign campaigns were imposed on imported luxuries. Throughout the time the King's German Legion was based in Bexhill smuggling was

41 *Martello Tower Number 47 and Coastguard Station on the Horn, c.1860. The view is from the entrance to a field off upper Belle Hill. The De La Warr Pavilion is now on the site of the Coastguard Station and the Colonnade on the site of the Martello Tower.*

42 *The Martello Tower on Galley Hill, 1863. The view is from Little Galley Hill across Glyne Gap. Note the lagoon behind the beach.*

going on all around them. Smuggling account books have been discovered for both the Gillham family of Little Common and the Pocock family of Bexhill. Besides goods being smuggled in, spies, letters and newspapers were smuggled out of the country by the same route. The passage of time has allowed the subject to become romanticised but it was a brutal business that relied as much on fear and intimidation as on subterfuge. The *Sussex Advertiser* reported the murder of one of the soldiers of the King's German Legion at Little Common in 1805, possibly because he had discovered more than was good for him about Bexhill's black economy.

The local smuggling activities culminated in the so-called Battle of Sidley Green in 1828. Smugglers landed an illicit cargo on the beach, close to where the *Sackville* now stands. The Coast Blockade manning the Martello Tower on Galley Hill spotted but were unable to stop them and called for reinforcements. An eyewitness in the *Bell Hotel* later recalled a wounded smuggler being taken in and some cargo hidden. The Coast Blockade intercepted the smugglers at Sidley Green and a fierce fight ensued. There was one fatality on each side and many wounded. Eight smugglers were caught although the main force with the cargo escaped. The smugglers who were caught were eventually transported to Australia, which possibly explains the presence of a small village near Sydney called Bexhill.

Smuggling was brought under control by a reduction of the duty on imported goods and increased efficiency of enforcement. The Coast Blockade replaced the Preventive Men in 1818 and they were succeeded in turn by the Coastguard in 1831. The Martello Towers were used to control the coastline. Semaphore stations opened in 1820, allowing rapid communication; one was situated on the top of Galley Hill, one at Kewhurst and another near Martello Tower 55 at Normans Bay. Coastguard stations were built around the Martello Towers, at Cooden Beach, The Horn

43 *The New Inn, Sidley Green, c.1930. This was the site of the 'Battle of Sidley Green' between smugglers and the Coast Blockade in 1828.*

44 *Martello Tower Number 51, 1869. This drawing was made the year the tower collapsed. Tower 51 was situated on the shore near Culver Croft Bank, due south from Barnhorn.*

40

(now the site of the De La Warr Pavilion) and Galley Hill in the 1830s, and at Pevensey Sluice (Normans Bay) in 1866.

When the barracks were established a new cemetery was opened on Barrack Road. St Peter's churchyard alone would not have been large enough to cope with the additional burials associated with the influx of soldiers. Many members of the King's German Legion were buried at the Barrack Road cemetery. When the resort of Bexhill-on-Sea developed, a new cemetery was opened at Clinch Green in 1901, and an isolation hospital opened adjacent to it in 1902. During the Second World War the Barrack Road cemetery was bombed and most of the graves destroyed. It was taken over by Bexhill Corporation in 1965 and turned into a garden of rest.

The Down Mill, or Hoad's Mill as it became better known, stood on Gunters Lane. Although an 18th-century date has often been given for the mill, there is no evidence of its presence before 1810. From 1887 to 1987 the mill was owned and operated by the Hoad family. An electric motor was later installed to drive the millstones and the sweeps were no longer used. A storm in 1956 tore off one of the sweeps leaving the mill in a dilapidated state. The artist L.S. Lowry captured the look of the mill in its last years in his painting 'The Old Mill at Bexhill' in 1960. The main part of the mill finally collapsed in 1965, although the brick-built base has been preserved.

The opening line of Jane Austen's unfinished final novel *Sanditon* is, 'A gentleman and lady travelling from Tunbridge towards that part of the Sussex coast which lies between

45   *Bexhill Down, by Charles Graves, dated 1897. The Down Mill is on the skyline to the left.*

46 *Chantry Lane viewed from the bottom, c.1895. Chantry Lane runs from the old village of Bexhill to Holliers Hill and is deeply cut into the local sandstone, its tunnel-like character emphasised by the trees growing over the top. This would once have been part of the medieval 'King's Highway' from Bulverhythe to Sidley.*

Hastings and Eastbourne, being induced by business to quit the high road, and attempt a very rough lane, were overturned in toiling up its long ascent half rock, half sand.' Sanditon, geographically at least, appears to relate to Bexhill. Unfortunately the novel describes a fictional village and not Bexhill as it was when the novel was written in 1817. Elements of the book are prophetic, as Sanditon is described as being developed from a coastal village into a health-giving resort, something that did not occur in Bexhill until the 1880s.

Within Bexhill Museum's collections is a commemorative poster for an event on 4 June 1819 entitled 'A Remarkable instance of Longevity'. It records an assembly of 46 men at the *Bell Inn* to commemorate the 81st birthday of King George III. Of the 25 men who dined the average age was 81; of the 15 who waited at table the average age was 71; and of the six who rang the church bells the average age was 61. All of these men were selected from a male population of less than a thousand. The significance of the event was its indication that the inhabitants of Bexhill were healthy and long-lived, and it was the same health-giving properties of the area that later triggered the development of the seaside resort. Even today, a feature of the town is its attraction for those of retirement age. But in 1819 the community had no aspirations for major development and no established tourist economy to benefit from the display of the poster.

In 1813 Elizabeth Sackville married the 5th Earl De La Warr and brought together two very influential families, the Sackvilles and the Wests. The 5th Earl, George John West, took his wife's surname and put it in front of his own, the Wests thereby becoming Sackville-Wests. The West family had its own distinguished history; in 1610 Thomas West, the 3rd Baron De La Warr, brought food to the starving inhabitants of Jamestown in America and saved the colony; he became governor of Virginia and the state of Delaware is named after him.

The 5th Earl De La Warr became lord of the manor of Bexhill in 1865 and, after his death in 1869, Elizabeth Sackville-West became lady of the manor. Her husband, the 6th Earl De La Warr, became lord of the manor in 1870 and the 7th Earl succeeded in 1873. The 7th Earl De La Warr dropped the 'West' part of his surname in 1871, perhaps suggesting a split from the part of the family at Knole. It was thanks to the 7th Earl that Bexhill was transformed to the fashionable resort of Bexhill-on-Sea.

Before the development of the new resort there were several families of yeoman and gentry status in Bexhill. The Brooks, the Russells and the Dukes were all farmers and employers, related to each other by marriage. Arthur Brook moved to Bexhill from West Hoathly in West Sussex in the middle of the 18th century; he built Brook Lodge, now called The Grange, just before 1750 and died in 1782. His sons Stephen and Arthur remained in Bexhill, farming in partnership until 1824. Arthur bought Church Farm, also known as

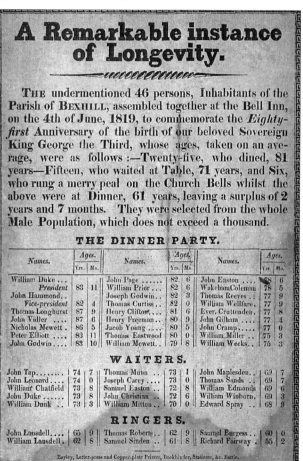

47 *A remarkable instance of longevity: poster, 1819.*

43

48 *Bexhill village from near the sheep wash at Brook Farm, 10 August 1866. Brook Farm was the Manor House. The farm track on the left leads into Manor House Farm.*

49 *Church Farm House, c.1910, viewed from the tower of St Peter's church. Church or Chantry Farm, as it was also known, was originally created to provide income as part of the endowment of the Batisford Chapel in St Peter's church in 1453.*

50 & 51 *Arthur Sawyer Brook, 'Squire' Brook, Master of the Bexhill Harriers, 'Arch-Tory and sometime king of Bexhill' c.1875; and Arthur John Brook, c.1880.*

Chantry Farm, in 1802 and Stephen bought Collington Farm. Arthur married Jane Russell and lived at the Manor House, or Court Lodge Farm, as it was then known. Their son, Arthur Sawyer Brook, known locally as 'Squire' Brook, was born in 1810; he married Ella Carswell in 1840 and died in 1890. They had two children, Ellen and Arthur John Brook, the latter a cricketer of some standing in the county.

The Brooks were a hunting family and were masters of the Bexhill Harrier pack from about 1785, 'Squire' Brook assuming the position

when his father died in 1835. The Prince of Wales joined one of the Harriers hunts in 1864 and, as a girl, Queen Victoria joined one of Brook's hunts in Bexhill. Brook was bailiff for Earl De La Warr and presided over the Court Leets. It is probable that it was this role that gave him the nickname of 'Squire'.

Sidley developed around crossroads in the local road network. The founding document of the Batisford Chantry in St Peter's church of 1456-7 mentions 'the King's Highway which leads from Bexle to Hastyngs' and 'the King's Highway that leads from Bexle to Sidlegh'.[3]

45

52 *Thatched cottage, Sidley, 1925. This building was set back to the side of the* Sussex Hotel. *It was demolished during the 1950s.*

From Bulverhythe the Hastings Road went to Bexhill village, then went across Holliers Hill to Sidley. At Sidley it continued inland to Ninfield and Lewes, but there was also Watermill Lane, leading to Catsfield and Battle, and Turkey Road, leading towards Barnhorn and the marsh. The *New Inn* and the forge would have been essential to travellers for rest, refreshment and re-shoeing horses. Sidley's first church was an iron structure dedicated to All Saints and opened in 1885; it was known as the 'Iron Church'. The current All Saints' church was consecrated in 1930. The Roman Catholic church of Our Lady of the Rosary opened in 1954.

Little Common takes its name from a triangular common including, and slightly larger than, the area between Green Lane and Lower Peartree Lane; at its apex is the Picknill Stream and at its base is the present-day A259. The common was designated 'waste of the Manor' during the late 18th and early 19th centuries, and enclosures were authorised. Cooden Down was one large common, the southern portion within the Manor of Cooden, the northern portion known as Slider's Common. An old Barnhorn rental refers to 'The Common of the Slyder in the Common of Coding'.

From the time of Queen Elizabeth I, and probably earlier, the highway between Hastings and Pevensey followed the lower marsh road, passing the 1455 Wallers Haven Sluice (where the *Star Inn* is situated). Travellers heading west by the coast road would have turned southwards at Little Common. Local traffic

46

53 Chimney Corner, Sidley, 1897 by F.H.H. A rare interior view of a local home at the end of the 19th century.

54 Sidley 'High Street', Ninfield Road at the junction with Turkey Road, 1909.

55   *Church Hill, Little Common, c.1910.*

increased dramatically during the Napoleonic Wars, and the village developed at this time. The *Wheatsheaf Inn* and various blacksmiths were once noticeably situated on the outside of a curve approached from the slightly higher and ancient Twitten.

The southern coast road was closed about 1876 when the sea encroached and blocked the area of the Cooden rail crossing. Traffic then followed what we now know as Old Marsh Road. Between 1929 and 1933 a new motor road was built across the marsh; this was in part a job creation scheme during the depression, but it did improve access to Bexhill.

The Methodist's 'Turf Chapel' of 1837 was Little Common's first place of worship, later to be rebuilt in brick in 1859. The current Methodist church was built in 1926 with the church hall added in 1953. St Mark's church was built using material recovered from Martello Tower No. 42, demolished in 1842. The parish of St Mark's was created in 1857 and the church enlarged in 1858. St Mark's Church of England School opened in 1855 and was extended in 1863 and 1890 as the population rose. The Catholic church of St Martha was opened in 1940 but not actually consecrated until 1971.

Five

THE 7TH EARL'S RESORT
OF BEXHILL-ON-SEA

In 1846 the railway came to, or rather past, Bexhill, the settlement being some distance north of the line. A simple country halt was built on the north side of the railway line, and a track linked the halt to Sea Lane, which then led up to Bexhill village. The track later became Station Road and also progressed west to connect with the lower part of the Belle Hill settlement. As the resort developed, Sea Lane became Sea Road, and the northern portion of Station Road became London Road. The railway sowed the seed for Bexhill's later development from village to town, but that development was not instantaneous.

The De La Warr estate owned much of Bexhill and it was the 7th Earl De La Warr who was responsible for creating the new resort of Bexhill-on-Sea. The Earl was a clergyman and had been chaplain to Queen Victoria between 1846 and 1865. He inherited the earldom following the tragic death of his brother by drowning in 1873.

There had been an earlier, failed attempt to create a new settlement in the Bexhill area. A plan of the proposed Pages Estate dated 1863 shows a development south of the *Denbigh Arms*. While none of the buildings was ever erected, part of the road network, including Collington Rise, was laid out. The plan also shows a seafront proposal at South Cliff, with a church and hotel. The exact date the *Denbigh Arms* was built is uncertain; it appears between 1840 and 1863 and was renamed the *Denbigh Hotel* in 1900. There is a connection between the Pages Estate plan and the *Denbigh*; either the settlement was going to be based around it or it was built in anticipation of the development. The first military unit recorded as being based at the Old Barracks arrived in July 1798, under the command of Lord Abervenny (short for Abergavenny), whose battalion included companies raised in Wales, notably one from Denbighshire. This suggests a possible reason for the *Denbigh Arms* name.

There were some changes during this post-railway, pre-resort period. A few houses were built on Station Road and Sea Road as Belle Hill and Bexhill village spread towards the railway halt. In 1866 the church of St James at Normans Bay was opened. In 1878 St Peter's church in Bexhill village was substantially altered, and the stonework revealed evidence of its Saxon origins.

The 7th Earl employed the building contractor John Webb to do most of the development work for him, and in part payment for his services he transferred to Webb a considerable portion of the new development: the land south of the railway line from Sea Lane westward as far as the Polegrove – much of what would now be considered central

56 *Reginald Windsor Sackville, 7th Earl De La Warr, by Frederick Sargent. (By courtesy of the National Portrait Gallery, London.)*

Bexhill. Webb's section of Bexhill was known as the Egerton Park Estate and it was agreed that it would include the majority of shops and services. The De La Warr Estate to the east was to be made up of large houses and fine hotels.

A street plan of Bexhill dated 1887 shows what the Earl intended the new resort to be like: a tidy, self-contained shopping area carefully confined to the west; a large pier extending out from the end of Sea Road; and a magnificent seafront from Sea Road to Galley Hill. Behind this were to be acres of high quality housing set in large gardens and ornamental parks. The plan also indicated which buildings were actually standing at

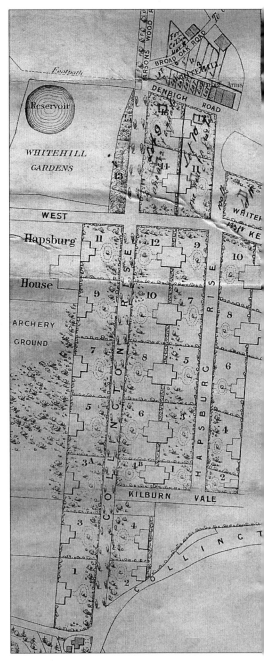

57 *Plan of the Pages Estate, 1863. This was never completed but part of the road layout was created. The Denbigh Arms is at the top of the plan.*

58 *The Metropolitan Convalescent Home from the patients' lawn, c.1938. This imposing building stood at the top of Upper Sea Road from 1881 to 1988.*

59 *Sackville Buildings, at the junction of Sackville Road and Wickham Avenue, 1898. This was the Sussex Dairy and Pritchard's Blind Makers, one of the first buildings in Sackville Road. To the left, houses on Cornwall Road can be seen.*

60 *Cooden Sea Road, c.1914. In the foreground is a cottage and tea garden. The top of Caledonia School on Clavering Walk can be seen above the roof of the cottage on the left. Metropolitan Convalescent Home for Men is in the distance on the right. Behind the house is the Cooden Beach Golf Course. The photograph is taken from the embankment of the railway line.*

that time, most of them on Webb's estate. The 7th Earl was never able to achieve his grand plan for Bexhill-on-Sea. Perhaps the most complete section of the town at this time was what is now London Road, on land belonging to Samuel Scrivens of Millfield; it formed the main shopping area before the shops in Devonshire Road and Sackville Road were opened.

Bexhill's first golf club was founded in 1880, the links occupying the eastern end of Earl De La Warr's estate. An old cottage on the site was used as the clubhouse and this was extended in 1912. The cottage is believed to have been a relic of the coal mining venture of 1805-10. However, the first major building development in Bexhill, and one causing some controversy at the time, was the Metropolitan Convalescent Institution, built on the brow of the hill in Bexhill village in 1881, for patients from London. It housed both men and women until 1905, when another Metropolitan Convalescent Institution was built in Cooden, leaving only women patients in Bexhill village. This project was followed by the construction of

the sea wall and the laying out of what is now East Parade in 1883.

The development of the resort was very rapid. Work began in 1883 and the town became an incorporated borough in 1902. In less than twenty years it was transformed from a small farming village to a town with ambitious plans for its future. The Ordnance Survey maps of Bexhill make the point very clearly: the 1873 map still strongly resembles the map made in about 1805 for the Duke of Dorset, save for the loss of the Martello Towers and the barracks and the addition of the railway line; the 1899 Ordnance Survey map, by comparison, shows a very different community. Suddenly a new town has appeared and where once there were only fields and scrubland there are now streets and houses.

Unlike most towns, where the railway line was built to fit into an established settlement, Bexhill-on-Sea had to be constructed around it. The railway still cuts the town centre in half, separating the Town Hall on the north side of the line from the shopping centre to the south. Because it was constructed through agricultural land in 1846, access from one

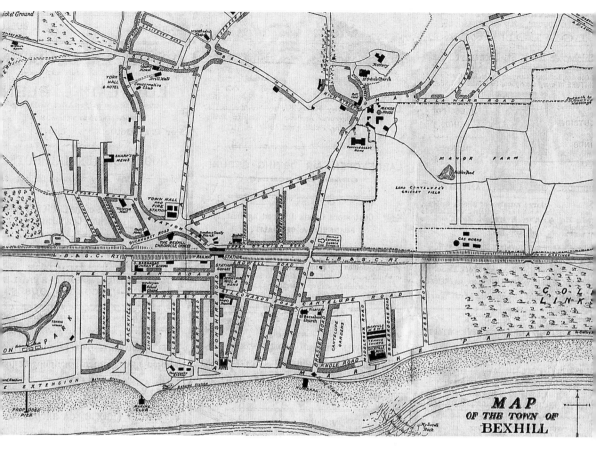

61   *Street map 1896. It shows a pier on West Parade that was never built.*

62   *Brooke's mineral water works, 'Western Road' 1909. The works were set back against the railway line. The building is now incorporated into The Mall but the back is still quite visible from Sainsbury's car park. At this time Western Road was mostly residential. The Western Road Garage later occupied the vacant plot to the left.*

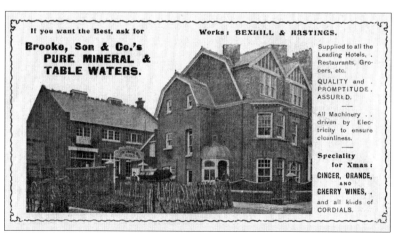

63 *The Farm Stores, Buckhurst Place, 1898. The site was cleared in 1974 and Sainsbury's supermarket opened there in 1976.*

64 *Fire brigade procession passing down Sackville Road, c.1932. Leading is the Merryweather steamer followed by Lady Kitty. In the background is St Barnabas' school, now Bexhill library.*

side of the line to the other was needed mainly for livestock. There was a bridge at Sea Road and cattle arches under the line at Sackville Road, Collington and Cooden. As Sackville Road became a major thoroughfare, the cattle arch created a bottleneck and it was demolished in 1892, replaced by a bridge carrying the line over the road. The new cast-iron bridge was made by the Pimlico foundry in London, owned by Henry Young who lived at Cooden Mount. This bridge was eventually replaced in 1978 by the current one. The construction of the Manor Road bridge over the railway line in 1928 helped to ease the growing congestion in the town as car ownership increased.

The growth of the new Bexhill-on-Sea was not a natural nor gradual expansion of the existing village; the resort was a new settlement and caused a massive influx of people into the area. The new town attracted traders and businessmen of all sorts and, in particular, became a centre for independent schools. A new railway station opened in 1891, facing onto what is now Devonshire Square but was then called Station Square. This station was short-lived and was replaced by the present station in 1902, the Devonshire Square station being too small to deal with the number of passengers travelling to the new resort.

There were early signs of a burgeoning spa town. The local spring water was greatly prized

65 *St Andrew's church, Wickham Avenue, c.1910. This opened as a mission church of St Barnabas in 1900.*

66 *Bexhill Down from Sutherland Avenue, c.1905. St Stephen's church is just visible on the skyline to the right.*

67 *Church of the Good Shepherd, Malet Hall, 20 March 1912. The church, on the first floor of the Malet Hall, is seen here decorated by the Young Leaguers.*

for its supposed health-giving properties, the 'chalybeate' or iron-rich spring water allegedly bottled for sale in London. John Lambert Walker, owner of the Woodsgate Park estate, constructed a covered well over a spring on his land near the junction of London Road and St George's Road. However, sea air and sea bathing soon took over as the main attraction for the resort and some of the hotels offered hydrotherapy and other treatments to attract convalescing visitors. Nevertheless, an attempt by the 8th Earl De La Warr to block the opening on the sea front of a convalescent home for consumptive patients suggests that rich hypochondriacs were more welcome than the genuinely ill.

Bexhill suffered a typhoid epidemic in August and September of 1880. It claimed 36 lives. The outbreak was blamed on contaminated wells and was one factor, along with the prospect of becoming a resort, which led to the establishment of the Local Board of Health in 1884; this would previously have been the responsibility 'of the Parish'.

In 1883 John Webb and two business associates petitioned to put forward a Parliamentary Bill to create a company for the supply of water and gas to the new town. This was opposed by the 7th Earl and his backers, who succeeded in blocking the Bill and then put forward one of their own, which was passed in 1885. Piped water became available to the town in 1887. John Webb laid out Egerton Park in 1888 to drain the surrounding land and make it suitable for building, and an open water tank was added in 1889 as the town's first swimming pool. The park and the promenade on West Parade were sold to Bexhill Urban District Council in 1901.

Bexhill gasworks opened on Ashdown Road in 1887 and in 1888 provided illumination for the streetlights; they closed in 1967. In 1900 street lighting changed over to electricity when the new electricity works opened next to the gasworks; Bexhill was said to be the first British town to supply electricity for domestic use. The Hastings gasworks were also within the boundary of Bexhill, and began production at Glyne Gap in 1907. The first telephone exchange opened in Devonshire Square in 1898, with 33 subscribers.

Bexhill's fire brigade was formed in 1888, its captain being Fred Russell of the Water and Gas Company. The men were volunteers and trained in the grounds of the gasworks until the first fire station was built in Endwell Road, partly on the site now occupied by the Post Office. In 1890 the brigade was taken over by the Urban District Council. A fire brigade competition was held in the grounds of the *Sackville Hotel* in 1891 and twice in 1892 in the Manor House grounds. As well as being entertainment, these events were the

source of much pride for the community. The brigade demonstrated their skills, for which prizes were awarded. The final competition in 1892 was ruined when Viscount Cantelupe announced that he would replace the captain of the fire brigade. They would not accept this and Cantelupe refused to give out the prizes. The result was that the volunteer fire brigade resigned. The brigade was reformed with only one of its original members and with Viscount Cantelupe as captain, and the fire station was moved to De La Warr Mews in Station Road. A horse and cart served as a temporary fire engine until a horse-drawn Merryweather Steamer was purchased in 1895. A new fire station was built behind the Town Hall on Amherst Road in 1896, and it remained there until 1971 when it was relocated to the corner of London Road and Beeching Road. During the First World War the army commandeered all available horses and Louis Russell of Russell's Garage not only modified a motor tractor to draw the steamer but also provided a lorry to act as a tender. In 1921 he fitted a motor pump to the lorry to create a unique fire engine, christened by Lady De La Warr in 1925 and

68 *Children from Nazareth House visit the St George's Cinema, March 1927.*

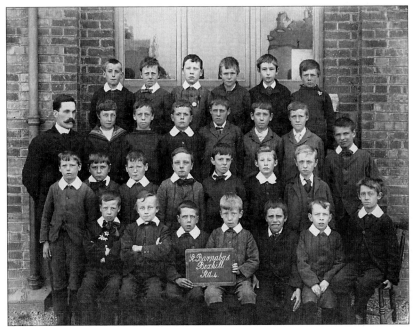

69 *St Barnabas'
boys school, Reginald
Road, June 1901.*

named 'Diana' after her. A second motor pump
was obtained in 1925 and with this Russell
created a smaller 'first aid' fire engine to
support 'Diana'. This was christened 'Helena'
in 1926 by Mrs Sewell, wife of the then mayor,
Councillor Sewell, who was also the chairman
of the Fire Brigade Committee. The next fire
engine was christened by and named after
the 9th Earl's daughter, 'Lady Kitty', in 1931.

The ancient parish church of St Peter's
became too small for the developing town and
a new parish was created when the church of
St Barnabas was built on Sea Road in 1890,
to be opened in 1891. St Andrew's church in
Wickham Avenue opened as a mission church
of St Barnabas in 1900, while the landowner
of Woodsgate Park, John Lambert Walker,
built St Stephen's church on Bexhill Down in
1900. This replaced the Down Mission Hall,
a simple iron hut built in 1885 that had been
poorly attended. Canadian soldiers training

at Cooden Camp during the First World
War later used the building as a canteen. The
Church of the Good Shepherd occupied the
first floor of the Malet Hall at the foot of
Belle Hill; the ground floor was the Malet
Memorial Institution. This was built in 1912
by Lady Ermyntrude Malet as a memorial to
her husband, Sir Edward Malet (1837-1908),
a high-ranking British diplomat who retired
to Bexhill. Wrest Wood, his mansion built in
1896-7, is now part of St Mary Wrestwood
Road School, a special needs school founded
in 1922. St Michael's church in Glassenbury
Drive was built in 1929 and St Augustine's in
Cooden Drive was started in 1933 but not
fully completed until 1963.

A Roman Catholic mission hall was built
in 1891 and the church of St Mary Magdalene
was opened next to it in 1907. Nazareth
House, sited prominently on Hastings Road,
was opened in 1894 as a home for the elderly,

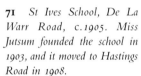

70 *Staff of the Down Secondary Modern School, 1960.*

71 *St Ives School, De La Warr Road, c.1905. Miss Jutsum founded the school in 1903, and it moved to Hastings Road in 1908.*

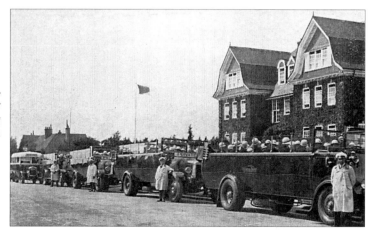

72 *St John's School for Girls, Collington Avenue, 1928. The char-a-bancs are preparing to take the pupils out on an excursion.*

73 *Advert for the* Castle Hotel, *Buckhurst Place, 1894. The hotel was built in 1886. The gap on the right of the* Castle *was the location of the Bijou Cinema that opened in 1910; this closed in 1954 and was demolished in 1993.*

74 *The* Granville Hotel, *Sea Road, c.1930.*

the poor and orphaned girls. It was extended in 1911 and a chapel added. In 1961 the Catholic school sited next to St Mary Magdalene's church since 1893 was removed to occupy a wing of Nazareth House.

The Methodist Parkhurst Hall opened in 1892 and was supplemented by the building of the adjoining Sackville Road church in 1896. Springfield Road Methodist church opened in 1907, the congregation of the Belle Hill Wesleyan chapel being amalgamated with it in 1938. The Beulah Baptist church on Buckhurst Road opened in 1898. Victoria Hall, a Congregationalist hall and school, was built on Victoria Road in 1887 and so-called because it opened

during Queen Victoria's golden jubilee. Next to this, facing onto London Road, St John's Congregationalist church was added in 1897. The Bexhill Corps of the Salvation Army was formed in 1892, holding open-air services and making use of various halls in the town. They were not initially well received and suffered from verbal and physical abuse. The foundation stone to their London Road Citadel was laid in 1914. The Quakers opened their Society of Friends Meeting House in Albert Road in 1965. St Paul's Free Church in Wickham Avenue began as a temporary wooden structure in 1924; a hall was added in 1931 and the current building opened on the site in 1963.

Commanding Unrivalled Position.
SACKVILLE HOTEL,

Bexhill-on-Sea, Sussex.
SOUTH ASPECT.

75 *Advert for the Sackville Hotel, 1894, which opened in 1890. This clearly shows the separation between the original hotel, on the left, and Sackville House, the Bexhill residence of the De La Warr family. The hotel was later extended to the north and to the east.*

Education has had an important role in the development and character of Bexhill. Dr Pye had created Bexhill's first known school in 1597 and there is also mention of a schoolmaster in 1775, but education did not become formally established until St Peter's School opened on Holliers Hill in 1853. This provided for the education of the poor, forming a girls department in 1862 and continuing in use until 1940. A St Peter's girls school and a St Peter's infants school were opened in Barrack Road in 1885, which incorporated the Wilson Memorial School, previously occupying a building at the western end of the barracks site. At this time education was still under the auspices of the parish church, much as it had been in Dr Pye's day. The

mid-19th-century expansion in the provision of schools was largely due to the work of the vicar of St Peter's church from 1840 to 1876, Henry Winckworth Simpson. In 1855 a schoolroom opened next to St Mark's church, Little Common and eventually developed into St Mark's School. This was replaced in 1961 by Little Common County Primary School and the old site was cleared to create the church's car park. All Saints' School in All Saints' Lane, Sidley was opened in 1865 and was used as a place of worship before the 'Iron Church' was built in 1885. Sidley County Primary School opened in Buxton Drive in 1951.

The 1870 Education Act made elementary education compulsory, and established local boards of education to provide it. However, Bexhill's educational needs were already met by the church, making the formation of a new board unnecessary. St Barnabas' girls and infants school opened in Western Road in 1893, and in 1898 St Barnabas' boys school opened in Reginald Road, the former site then dividing into girls upstairs and infants downstairs.

St Peter and St Paul School in Buckhurst Road was formally opened in 1956, replacing St Barnabas' boys and St Peter's girls schools. The building that had accommodated St Barnabas' girls school became the Bexhill public library in 1951. St Peter's girls school, in Barrack Road, became Chantry County Primary School.

Under the 1902 Education Act a Local Education Committee was formed. This created the Down Elementary School, now King Offa County Primary School, which opened in 1907 and was extended in 1912. The Down Secondary School, situated behind the Down School, and now Bexhill High School, was planned as part of a reorganisation of elementary education in 1930 but was not opened until 1941 when evacuees returned to the town, the whole site re-opening in 1943.

The adjoining Bexhill Boys Grammar School and Bexhill Girls Grammar School in Turkey Road, Sidley were completed in 1926 and formally opened in 1927. They amalgamated in September 1970 to create the Bexhill Grammar School, the site later becoming Bexhill Sixth Form College. St Richard's Roman Catholic College, which serves a large catchment area beyond Bexhill, opened in Ashdown Road in 1959.

To meet the needs of the new developments on the eastern side of Bexhill, Pebsham County Primary School was created. This began as two mobile classrooms in Chantry County Primary School in 1977 but moved to new premises at the start of 1977. Glyne Gap Special School opened in 1970.

One of the most unusual features of the town was the number of independent schools that were established or relocated here. Bexhill became a major scholastic centre and the presence of the schools made an important contribution to the town's economy. There were far too many schools to name them all, but they included institutions such as Charters Towers, Ancaster House, The Beehive, Normandale and St John's School. There have been about 180 different independent schools, catering for all ages, based in Bexhill since the development of the resort.

A vital part of any resort is the provision of high quality accommodation, and the fortunes of the town can be followed through the fate of its hotels. The *Castle Hotel* in Buckhurst Place and the *Devonshire Hotel* in Devonshire Road were both opened in

76   *The unveiling of the Lane Memorial, Buckhurst Place, 25 June 1898. The Farm Stores and railway line can be seen in the background; this is now the site of Sainsbury's supermarket.*

77 *Town Hall Square, Buckhurst Place, c.1901. On the left is the Town Hall, built in 1894 and opened by the Lord Mayor of London in 1895. Next to it is the London and Counties Bank, which opened in 1898. In the middle is the Lane Memorial, commemorating the life and service to the town of Lt. Col. Henry Lane (1827-95), 'Father of Local Government in Bexhill'. This was unveiled on 25 June 1898 by his widow, assisted by Lord Brassey and Earl De La Warr.*

1886. John Webb built the latter and was its first licensee. The *York Hotel* in London Road was built in 1895 and next to it the York Hall. Of the town's more prestigious hotels, the third grandest was the *Granville Hotel* on Sea Road, completed by 1902 but unable to begin operating until 1905 due to licensing problems. The second grandest was the *Metropole Hotel*, opened on the sea front at the end of Sackville Road in 1900. The most luxurious place to stay in the new resort was the *Sackville Hotel* on De La Warr Parade. When it opened in 1890 the eastern half of the building was still the private residence of Earl De La Warr's family in Bexhill.

Bexhill Urban District Council, or Bexhill District Council as it was also known, was formed in 1894. Lieutenant-Colonel Henry Lane (1827-95) was its first chairman, having been chairman of the preceding Local Board. His influential role in the early years of the resort was acknowledged by his epitaph 'Father of Local Government in Bexhill', and a memorial to him was erected in Buckhurst Place (Town Hall Square). After his death, the Viscount Cantelupe, son and heir to the 7th Earl De La Warr, continued as chairman of Bexhill Urban District Council. Viscount Cantelupe became the heir to the De La Warr title following the death of his elder brother in a yachting accident.

Six

THE 8TH EARL
DE LA WARR

78   *Viscount and Muriel Cantelupe, c.1892, a pair of portraits taken shortly after their marriage in 1891, perhaps within the Manor House where they lived.*

Bexhill and Dunlop

In 1891 the Earl's son and heir, Gilbert George Reginald Sackville, the Viscount Cantelupe, married Muriel Brassey, bringing together two very important families. Muriel was the daughter of Lord Brassey and Annie Lady Brassey, who were Victorian *nouveaux riches*. Lord Brassey's father was Thomas Brassey, the great railway contractor who, on his death, was estimated to be worth £5 million and Annie's

father and grandfather were both successful wine merchants. Annie Brassey was famous as a writer, traveller and collector. She wrote eight books, the best known being *A Voyage in the Sunbeam*, describing the circumnavigation of the globe made by the family aboard their steam yacht *Sunbeam* in 1876-7.

The 7th Earl De La Warr had transferred control of the Bexhill estate to his son soon

65

79 *Sir Thomas Brassey (1836-1918) in around 1878. He was the son of Thomas Brassey (1805-70), the great Victorian railway contractor, husband of Annie Lady Brassey, and grandfather of the 9th Earl De La Warr. Thomas received his knighthood in 1881, became Baron Brassey of Bulkeley in 1886 and Earl Brassey in 1911. His career included being Liberal MP for Hastings 1868-81, Civil Lord of the Admiralty 1880-4, Lord Warden of the Cinque Ports 1908-13, Lord-in-Waiting to Queen Victoria 1893-5 and Governor of Victoria, Australia 1895-1900. Thomas Brassey presented Bexhill Borough Council with its mayoral chain and gavel in 1906 and was himself mayor of Bexhill from 1907-8.*

after his marriage. Viscount and Lady Cantelupe first lived at Sackville House, the private east end of the *Sackville Hotel*, while the Manor House was refurbished for their use. It has been stated that some £15,000 was spent on the Manor House in 1891; it was fitted with modern conveniences such as electricity and a telephone. After the couple moved into their new home in 1892, the Manor House and its extensive grounds became a focus for the town's social and sporting events.

In 1894 and 1895 Viscount Cantelupe attempted to sell East Parade to Bexhill Urban District Council, but they were not prepared to pay the price asked. Cantelupe reacted by building the De La Warr gates at the entrance to East Parade, or De La Warr Parade as it was renamed. The gates were more symbolic than practical but they clearly defined the boundary of the Earl's Bexhill estate, the development and promotion of

which he became personally involved with. There was another dispute between the town and the Earl in 1895 over a piece of land which came to be known as the Triangular Plot. This is now the eastern end of the De La Warr Pavilion car park and was then used as a public open space. It was still in the Earl's possession but was isolated from the rest of his property. He allowed the local authority, the Bexhill Board, to have the land for a peppercorn rent on the understanding that it was properly maintained, but claimed it was not being looked after, and took it back at the end of 1895. He subsequently sold it to the developer Mr Gold, who built Marina Court, a large apartment block, on the site, which opened in 1901.

The Town Hall was built in 1894 and opened in April 1895 by Sir Joseph Renals, the Lord Mayor of London, his state coach and horses being brought to Bexhill by train for the event. Sir Joseph and Lady Renals were personal friends of Viscount and Lady Cantelupe and stayed with them at the Manor House.

The 7th Earl De La Warr died in 1896 and the Viscount Cantelupe succeeded as the 8th Earl. While the 7th Earl had started the development of Bexhill at the end of his life, the 8th Earl took it over during the prime of his; however, the 8th Earl's youth and enthusiasm were not tempered by prudence or experience.

The 8th Earl built a new entertainment pavilion on East Parade in 1896. It was named the Kursaal, a German word for the entertainment pavilion at a spa. The Kursaal was intended to be a pier, but only the landward section was ever built, although it did project over the top of the beach and was accessed

80 *Top right: Annie Lady Brassey, c.1878, on board the steam yacht* Sunbeam. *Mother of Muriel, Countess De La Warr and grandmother of the 9th Earl De La Warr, Annie died at sea in 1887 and only saw the resort of Bexhill-on-Sea during its earliest years, but her family was to have great local significance.*

81 *Right: The Lord Mayor of London, Sir Joseph Renals, turning off Devonshire Road into Western Road in his state coach, 27 April 1895. The Lord Mayor visited Bexhill to open the Town Hall.*

82 *The De La Warr Gates, at the entrance to De La Warr Parade, c.1900.*

83 *Marina, 1901. On the left, Marina Arcade is under construction. In the middle is Marina Court, the* Metropole Hotel *visible behind and to its right. To the right of Marina Arcade is Roberts Marine Mansions, and on the far right is the corner of the* Wilton Court Hotel. *Part of the De La Warr Gates can be seen on the right-hand side.*

from the promenade. In 1900 James Glover was appointed as manager. He was also the Musical Director at Drury Lane and this allowed him to book the very best artistes in the country to perform at the Kursaal. The domes and 'orientalist' style of the building, popular elsewhere at this time, set the trend for the sea front. Marina Arcade was built in 1901, originally planned as a lavish swimming pool complex but never completed as such. There was also a plan to build a pier from the site; indeed, Channel View East and Channel View West on either side of Marina Arcade were for a while known as Pier View East and Pier View West. The next block to the west is Marina Court Avenue, which was built between 1902 and 1908.

The oriental style of these bungalows has given rise to one of Bexhill's most enduring myths, that they were built by the Maharajah of Cooch Behar as a seraglio for his harem; the story is sometimes embellished with the suggestion that each front door had a different design of doorknocker so the Maharajah knew which wife was where. Nripendra, Maharajah of Cooch Behar did indeed stay at 22 Marina Court Avenue during the summer of 1911, but he came here on the advice of his doctor to regain his failing health. As a follower of the Brahmo Samaj religion he was monotheistic and monogamous, thus dispelling the harem story. Despite Bexhill's regenerative climate the Maharajah died. The funeral procession that passed from Marina Court Avenue to

84 *The opening of the Kursaal by the Duchess of Teck in 1896.*

85 *Kursaal programme, c.1901.*

the railway station on 21 September 1911 was Bexhill's largest state occasion. The Maharajah's family showed their appreciation for the respect shown to him by building a memorial fountain on the coastguard station

behind the Colonnade. Maharajah Jitendra unveiled it in 1913, the only feature in Bexhill actually built by the Maharajahs of Cooch Behar.

Another of the 8th Earl's innovations was the construction of a Bicycle Boulevard on De La Warr Parade in 1896. On the promenade near to the *Sackville Hotel* was a cycle chalet where payment for the use of the track was made, bicycles were hired and lessons in riding given. From the chalet the track extended east to a turn around point at the foot of Galley Hill. Cycling was a craze of the 1890s and the Earl took full advantage of it to promote his new resort. International cycling tournaments were held in the grounds of the Manor House in 1896 and 1897, the Grand Duke Michael of Russia and his wife the Countess de Torby attending the latter. The Bexhill Cycling Club, founded in 1889, took over the organisation of the event and held a Cycling Tournament and Athletic Meeting in Egerton Park in 1898. Other guests at the 1896 event included Ernest Terah Hooley, 'Company Promoter', and Alexander Meyrick Broadley, 'The Pasha', two men who were to get the Earl into deep financial trouble.[1] Hooley 'promoted' the Dunlop Pneumatic Tyre Company, French Dunlop, Bovril and Schweppes; Broadley introduced the 8th Earl to Hooley in 1896 and offered him directorship of the Dunlop Company. De La Warr accepted and also persuaded other peers to join the board. The Earl recruited the Duke of Somerset and the Earl of Albemarle and was paid for his services. Despite his inexperience, De La Warr joined the boards of other companies promoted by Hooley, including the Bovril Company. It all went badly wrong in 1898 when Hooley became bankrupt and the 8th Earl had to

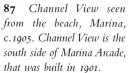

86 *Central Parade, c.1910. To the left is Marina Arcade, built in 1901, in the background is Marina Court that opened in 1901 and on the right is Roberts Marine Mansions, formerly the Marine Hotel built in 1895. In the foreground is the weather station.*

87 *Channel View seen from the beach, Marina, c.1905. Channel View is the south side of Marina Arcade, that was built in 1901.*

88 *The opening of the Maharajah of Cooch Behar's memorial fountain by the then Maharajah Jitendra, 18 September 1913. Jitendra was the second son of Maharajah Nripendra, who died in Bexhill in 1911. The Memorial was behind the Colonnade; Marina Court can be seen in the background.*

89 *Staff at the Bicycle Boulevard's Cycle Chalet, De La Warr Parade, c.1896. The Sackville Hotel is in the background.*

90 *Races at the 1897 Cycle Tournament, held in the Manor House grounds. The Convalescent Home is in the background.*

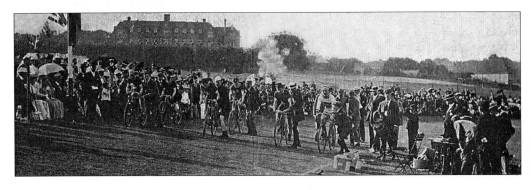

promise in court to pay back the thousands of pounds he had been given. Financially the Earl never recovered and the matter dealt a serious blow to his reputation. The Earl also had other problems, Lady De La Warr finding out that he had been unfaithful to her and the marriage nearly ending; however she decided to forgive him, due to the stress that he had suffered.

In 1899 the Earl took a job as a war correspondent for *The Globe* magazine, and left for South Africa to cover the Second Boer War. While he was away Lady De La Warr gave birth to their third child and only son, Herbrand, the future 9th Earl. In 1900 the 8th Earl was wounded during a battle as he attempted to rescue an injured soldier, and he returned that July to a hero's welcome. For a while life at the Manor House returned to normal, but by Christmas 1901 the 8th Earl had begun an affair with an actress at the Kursaal, a Miss Turner. He did not return to his young family but continued his involvement with the developing resort.

91 *Bicycle Boulevard, De La Warr Parade, c.1901. The Hotel Riposo on the left was opened in 1901 and demolished in 1961; the site is now occupied by Cavendish Court.*

92 *'Bexhill and Dunlop', the Spy cartoon of 1896 depicting the 8th Earl De La Warr. The title refers to the Earl's main business interests, promoting his resort and the pneumatic tyre company of which he was a director. In 1891 he married Muriel Brassey, daughter of the famous Annie Lady Brassey.*

93 *De La Warr Parade, 1900, awaiting the 8th Earl's return from the Boer War. On the left is the Kursaal and telegraph office kiosk; the De La Warr Gates can be seen in the distance.*

Edwardian Bexhill — fast cars and scandal

Bexhill has been described as an Edwardian resort but most of the town was built during the late Victorian period. The town's first omnibus service was started by Mr Bradney Williams in 1901, very early for a bus service and an indication that motorised transport was to become a feature of Bexhill. The same year is also said to be the one in which Bexhill became the first English resort to

94 *The beach below Sea Road, c.1905. Marina Arcade is in the background to the left. The striped tents were used for changing, the bathing stations charged for their services and the only place where swimming was free at this time was West Parade because it was still undeveloped.*

95 *The start of Britain's first ever motor car race, Galley Hill, 19 May 1902.*

permit mixed bathing, although it is known that mixed bathing had been taking place at Cromer since 1898. There is as yet no evidence to support the 1901 claim, and in fact mixed bathing may have been a regular occurrence in Bexhill before this. Also in 1901 the Artillery Drill Hall was built on Bexhill Down, and a second drill hall for the Territorial Army was build next to it on the western side in 1915.

The following year was perhaps the most eventful year in the history of the town. Bexhill became an incorporated borough and elected its first mayor, a branch line and three new railway stations opened, and the town hosted Britain's first ever motor car race.

On 3 May 1902 Mr Williams, the man who had created the bus service, bought a 12-horsepower Argyll car in Glasgow and began a motor reliability run by driving it back to Bexhill. This car was later to be used during the town's Incorporation celebrations. Gustavus Green opened workshops in Reginald Road. He had moved to Bexhill, aged 32, in 1896, and established a bicycle-making business at 5 Western Road to capitalise on the cycling craze. He designed a water-cooled motor car engine, which was later converted for use in aircraft. Green's famous engines were also used to power torpedo boats.

Bexhill's 'Great Whitsuntide Motor Races' were held on De La Warr Parade on 19 May 1902. The 8th Earl had encouraged the Automobile Club of Great Britain and Ireland to organise the event on his private land, which was exempt from the national speed limit of 12 miles an hour. The Earl turned his bicycle track into the country's first motor racing venue and a course of one kilometre was

96 *Officials inspecting Britain's first motor racing track, De La Warr Parade, Bexhill-on-Sea. This was taken at 6 a.m. on the morning of 19 May 1902. The 8th Earl De La Warr is on the left.*

97 *The Crowhurst viaduct in about 1902.*

set out. The unit of measurement indicates that motor racing was a French innovation; Earl De La Warr had seen cars racing on the sea front at Nice in 1901 and in 1902. His was an international event, with drivers coming from the continent to compete. The races were won by the French driver Leon Serpollet in his steam car Easter Egg, which reached a speed of 55 miles per hour. The races did not delight everyone. Mr Mayner, who owned property on De La Warr Parade, took out a permanent injunction against the use of the road for races as it blocked his tenants' access, and the races planned for June had to be called off. The injunction did not end all of the year's motoring events. When the local troops returned from South Africa on 18 June 1902 they were driven back to their homes by motor car. On 6 September 1902 the Great Motor Reliability

Trials finished at Bexhill, culminating with lunch at the *Sackville Hotel*.

The excitement of the races had barely died down when they were followed by celebrations to mark the incorporation of Bexhill as a borough. Work had begun in 1899 to achieve borough status and so endorse the success of the growing town. The royal charter was the first to be granted by Edward VII and Bexhill was the last Sussex town to be incorporated. Appropriately the royal charter was also the first to be delivered by motor car. On 21 May it was brought down to Bexhill by train but collected at the station by the 8th Earl in Mr Bradney Williams' Argyll car, which led a procession to the Town Hall where the charter was read to an expectant crowd. The Earl had been named as provisional mayor on the draft charter but he was to be disappointed.

Bexhill needed better access if it were to flourish and this was achieved on 31 May 1902 when the Crowhurst branch line opened. This was a major engineering feat, requiring the construction of the Crowhurst Viaduct, or the 'Seventeen Arches' as it was known locally. The line started at the Bexhill West Station on Terminus Road, ran through the hamlet of Sidley, where a station was built, and joined the main line at Crowhurst. The journey time to London was reduced to about an hour and a half, saving an hour on a round trip.

With the opening of the Crowhurst line, Sidley was easily accessible for the first time. Sidley railway station and two new hotels opened to accommodate the influx of visitors: the *Pelham Hotel* opposite the station, and the *Sussex Hotel* on Ninfield Road. The latter replaced the earlier *Sussex Inn*, which had occupied the site next to it. The centre of village life was, and continues to be, the *New Inn*, one of the original staging posts for coaches. The earliest references to the *New Inn* are in the mid-18th century,

when it was called the *Five Bells*. Sidley was a small agricultural settlement of farmers and those trades and businesses which supported farming: blacksmiths, butchers and millers. It had three windmills, the last to survive being Pankhurst's Mill on Ninfield Road, built in about 1813 and dismantled in 1928. Sidley became a focus of brick-making when the new resort was being built. Adam's brickyard and the Highwoods brickyard were important sources of local employment.

The new resort of Bexhill-on-Sea was to gain a new railway station appropriate to its burgeoning size and ambitions, Bexhill Central Station, built facing onto Sea Road. Providing convenient access to both the Webb and De La Warr estates and opened on 30 June 1902, it was not, however, where the Earl had wanted the station to be located. A town map of 1900 shows it drawn in at the far end of East Parade, where Sutton Place now stands; this would have given direct access to the Earl's estate but have been highly inconvenient for the rest of the town. The Central Station

98 *The first train to arrive at the Bexhill West railway station, 31 May 1902.*

99   Sackville Hotel's *carriage outside the Bexhill West Station, c.1910.*

is remarkable for the length of the platforms extending from the old Devonshire Square station site up to the ticket office on Sea Road, almost the entire length of Endwell Road. It still stands as testament to the vast numbers of people who came to the town during its heyday; thousands of well-to-do visitors would stay for weeks or months during the summer season and, as they were leaving, thousands of schoolchildren would be arriving to start a new term. There have been over three hundred schools in Bexhill, largely independent boarding schools; many of the pupils were children of the colonial administration and armed forces overseas, who found the town to be a safe and healthy place for their children to be educated. High-class tourism and independent education were the main sources of the town's prosperity.

Despite the Earl's prominence in the events of 1902, he was not with his family at the Manor House; at the start of the year he had taken an apartment at Marina Court, on the sea front. His domestic problems must have been a topic of conversation throughout the year but the situation came to a head on 19 July when *The Times* reported his divorce and printed a letter in which he confessed his adultery to his wife. Muriel, Lady De La Warr, was granted custody of the children.

100 *A hot and busy summer's day on De La Warr Parade, c.1900. The view is from the deck of the Kursaal looking east; on the left is the bandstand. This provides an excellent view of the first seawall that was built by John Webb in 1883.*

The town celebrated the coronation of King Edward VII on 9 August 1902 with processions, bonfires, fireworks, athletic events and a dinner on Sidley Green for elderly residents. A permanent memorial to the coronation was planned, a clock tower on West Parade, but, due to a combination of bad luck and poor planning, it was not completed until 1904.

The charter of incorporation allowed for the election of a town council and a mayor, and Bexhill's first elections were held in November 1902. The 8th Earl De La Warr was still dogged by the scandal of his divorce and was not elected as mayor; that honour went to Ebenezer Howard. The 8th Earl remarried on 20 September 1903, not Miss Turner, the actress from the Kursaal, but Hilda Mary Clavering, the daughter of Colonel C. Lennox Tredcroft, the senior trustee of the De La Warr estate. The Earl's ambition to be mayor of Bexhill was delayed rather than defeated and he was successfully elected in November 1903.

Muriel, Lady De La Warr, gave up the Manor House and went to live with her father Earl Brassey at Normanhurst Court, Catsfield; Sackville Lodge was built on the

101 *The Clock Tower and bandstand on West Parade, c.1910. The Clock Tower was designed to commemorate the coronation of King Edward VII in 1902 but was not completed until 1904. While most of the resort was developed by this time, there are still very few buildings on West Parade.*

102 *'The Day of My Life', a* Bexhill Observer *cartoon satirising the 8th Earl De La Warr's election as mayor in 1903. Jour De Ma Vie is the De La Warr family motto. The Earl is shown riding in triumph on a motor-powered hobbyhorse equipped with Dunlop tyres. Leading the procession is Jimmy Glover, manager of the Kursaal. Behind the Earl and holding his train is Alderman Vale; carrying a fan is Daniel Mayer; holding a cricket bat is Councillor Howard; Councillor Lawrence, the chairman of the Education Board, is dressed as a teacher; behind him is Alderman Smith, and finally Alderman Henry Young. (By A. Stanley Young.)*

103 *Cars racing up Galley Hill during the 1904 motor car races.*

104 *An unusual view from the 1904 motor speed trails. The cars processing around the town centre are turning from Marina into Devonshire Road. On the left is Marina Court, clearly showing the shops along its north frontage, next to this are the Coastguard Cottages, and beyond this the Metropole Hotel.*

top of Galley Hill at this time and it was reputed to be a residence for her in Bexhill. In 1903 the Manor House was leased to August Neven Du Mont, the son of the owner of *Kolnische Zeitung*, a Cologne newspaper. Du Mont created what is now the Manor Barn as a ballroom and theatre for amateur dramatics. Mrs Du Mont opened a German school, The Deutsches Paedagogium, which had among its pupils a nephew of the Kaiser. August Du Mont also encouraged the talent of two young writers and illustrators, Joyce and Nina Brisley, daughters of George Brisley who ran a chemist shop in London Road. Joyce and Nina started by contributing work to the *Bexhill Observer* from 1911, and went on to become established authors and illustrators of children's books. Joyce in particular became best known for her Milly-Molly-Mandy stories, published from 1928 onwards.

Despite the permanent injunction against racing on the sea front there were further motor-related events. Another Motor Reliability Trial was arranged to finish in Bexhill, but the participants were unable to restrain themselves and the cycle track was once more used for speed trials. That the injunction was not used to stop this, or later events, suggests that some agreement was reached with Mr Mayner; he had previously entered into a contract with the Earl to construct a number of high quality buildings on the sea front but was unable to meet these obligations, so perhaps overlooking the injunction was his way out. Speed trials were held from 1904 to 1907. In 1922 there were speed trials on West Parade and again in 1923. Even in 1902 there had been concerns over the suitability of the sea front for racing, since it was not straight and there was hardly enough room to decelerate

105 *Egerton Park Pergola, c.1920. The Pergola started as an open-air stage built in 1906, and was partially enclosed in 1909. During 1932-3 it was replaced by the Egerton Park Pavilion, a combined theatre and indoor bowling green.*

106 *A tram passing down Devonshire Road, c.1908. The building on the right is Roberts Marine Mansions; built in 1895, it was demolished in 1954 and replaced by Dalmore Court in 1961.*

before the De La Warr Gates. As cars became faster the problems were compounded. What was needed was a racing circuit and one was proposed in 1906. The National Motor Course Company produced plans for an eight-mile course across the Pevensey Levels with loops at Cooden Beach and Pevensey a whole year before Brooklands opened, and if it had been built Bexhill would have been the home as well as birthplace of British motor sport. Concours d'Elegance car shows offered a safer alternative to racing, and were held on East Parade in 1934 and 1935, with a final one in 1936 on the terrace of the then newly opened De La Warr Pavilion.

The resort's police station and magistrates court were opened in Cantelupe Road in 1903. The first police station had been in Barrack Road, following the establishment of the Sussex Constabulary in 1840, and it was also the home of the police sergeant and the lock-up for prisoners. The facilities in Egerton Park were enhanced by the opening of the Shelter Hall in 1903, providing public toilets and creating an indoor venue for entertainment in the park. Egerton Park was extended by four acres in 1906 to bring it up to the present boundary at Brockley Road; Sir W. Vaughan Morgan, Lord Mayor of London, performed the opening ceremony. The Lord Mayor and his retinue stayed at the *Metropole Hotel.* The park extension included an open-air stage, partially enclosed in 1909 to form the Egerton Park Pergola. This was rebuilt in 1932-3 as the Egerton Park Pavilion and included the Egerton Park Theatre.

Public transport continued to improve. A motor train service began between St Leonards and Eastbourne in 1905, a shuttle service using a combined engine and carriage. New halts were built at Glyne Gap, Collington, Cooden Beach and Normans Bay. Part of the recently proposed regeneration package for the area included a similar service and the reinstatement of a station at Glyne Gap. Bexhill's tram service began in 1906, the tramline running from West Marina in St Leonards to outside the *Metropole Hotel*. Later in 1906 it was extended to Cooden Beach. In 1928 the trams were replaced by a trolleybus service. These used the overhead power lines but did not require tramlines, which were subsequently removed. There was a trolleybus turning circle at what is now the Sackville Road roundabout and another outside the *Cooden Beach Hotel*. The last trolleybus ran from Bexhill to Hastings in June 1959.

The artist Albert Goodwin (1845-1932) lived for many years at Ellerslie in Bexhill. He moved here with his family in 1906 and stayed for the rest of life. His daughters Olive and Christabel stayed on at Ellerslie; in the 1930s Christabel (1884-1971) ran the Highwoods Pottery and made decorative ceramic pots and tiles. Highwoods Pottery was situated at the entrance to the brick works on Turkey Road.

In 1907 Bexhill received its official coat-of-arms, which includes the emblems of the Earls De La Warr, a black star, and the Brasseys, a mallard duck. The bishops of Chichester are represented by a mitre and the Cinque Ports connection, albeit small, the demi-hulk emblem. Eight small birds or 'martlets' surround the coat-of-arms, the emblems of Sussex, while a helmet bearing a Martello Tower surmounts the whole. Below the coat-of-arms is the town motto 'Sol et Salubritas', 'Sun and Health', aptly

107 *Sea Road, c.1923. The tram tracks turning into Endwell Road can be seen in the foreground.*

108 *Cooden Beach, c.1910. The building behind the children is the Little Tea House.*

109 *The Bexhill coat-of-arms, the grant of which was made in 1907. The motto means 'Sun and Health'.*

chosen for promoting the young resort. The town colours of red, green and white had been chosen, with the help of Lady De La Warr, in 1893 at the formation of the rowing club.

Central Parade was developed in 1910 and the low sandy cliff known as The Horn was landscaped to form a bandstand. In 1911 the bandstand was transformed into the Colonnade to commemorate the Coronation of King George V. The Promenade originally extended around the Colonnade over the beach on a pier-like walkway, so that passers-by would not disturb the concerts, but this, like the central bandstand, has since been lost.

The Kursaal had been the first venue in Bexhill to show moving pictures, with a velograph of Gladstone's funeral in 1898. From 1900 films became a semi-regular part of the Kursaal's programme. Harry Collard and Pat Kinsella managed the first purpose-built

cinema, The Bijou, which was constructed in Buckhurst Place next to the *Castle
Hotel* in 1910. Collard and Kinsella had an
established reputation in Bexhill, running
and performing with the concert party The
Coronets, who also performed at the Bijou.
Local events were filmed and then shown. The
Bijou was modernised in 1912 in preparation
for new competition, the opening of the
Cinema-de-Luxe in Western Road in 1913.
The Bijou underwent many name changes
but, as the Savoy, finally closed in 1954; the
building was demolished in 1993. The owners
of the Cinema-de-Luxe developed the site
next door, opening the Picture Playhouse in
1921, when the Cinema-de-Luxe was closed.

110 *Drawing of the Bexhill Rowing Club's combined clubhouse and boathouse, situated on the west
side of The Horn, c.1894. Unfortunately this elegant
building burnt down in 1900.*

111 *Central Parade, just after it was completed in 1910. The temporary bandstand constructed on The Horn was
replaced by the Colonnade in 1911.*

Daimler "Silent Knight" Cabriolets for Hire.

The "Last Word" in Hire Cars.

CAN BE ENTIRELY CLOSED LIKE A LANDAULETTE OR OPEN.

MOTOR AMBULANCE, TAXI CABS AND PRIVATE LANDAULETTES FOR HIRE.

SOLE AGENT for this District for the well-known "FORD" CARS

H. PULHAM & CO'S FAMOUS FORD COACH, with Ford Chassis and local built body, which was running all last season, and which is still in the best of condition. The Engine and Chassis are the same as are used for the £135 Car.

275,000 Ford Cars already sold during the life of the Ford organization—Runabouts. £125 (dickey seat to carry two £1 extra); Five-passenger Touring Car, £135; Town Car, £185—complete with full equipment: Head lamps, side and tail lamps, speedometer, horn, hood, wind screen, tyre pump, repair outfit, two levers, tools and jack. Full particulars from . . .

THE INTERESTING CAR.

The "Ford Times" for November (a monthly publication of the Ford Motor Company) contains a picture of Pulham's Ford Coach, with the Coronets' party on board. The "Times" says:—"We expressly disassociate ourselves from the body of the car, which is not ours. We expressly associate ourselves with the chassis, which is a Ford in daily service for hire work at Pulham's, of Bexhill. As for the car contents or some of it, with a special exclusive work for the mascot on the bonnet—why, we express no opinion."

H. PULHAM & CO.,
Sackville Road Garage, Bexhill-on-Sea.

Telephone 399.   Telephone 399.

Ford
THE UNIVERSAL CAR

112 *Promenade and Colonnade Bandstand, c.1911. Earl Brassey opened the Colonnade in 1911.*

113 *Advert for H. Pulham & Co.'s Sackville Road Garage, 1913. Illustrated is a Pulham's Ford Coach; in it are the Coronets concert party. In the front seat are Harry Collard and Pat Kinsella (driving). A quote from the* Ford Times *says: 'We expressly disassociate ourselves from the body of the car, which is not ours. We expressly associate ourselves with the chassis, which is a Ford in daily service for hire work at Pulham's, of Bexhill. As for the car contents, or some of it, with a special exclusive work for the mascot on the bonnet – why, we express no opinion.'*

The ground floor was converted for bingo in 1974 but the cinema continues to function on the first floor. Now known as the Curzon Picture Playhouse, it is Bexhill's last remaining cinema. In 1935 the York Hall in London Road became the Gaiety Cinema, which was bombed in 1940 and never reopened. Bexhill's largest cinema was the Ritz, which opened in Buckhurst Road in 1937. The site was originally a roller-skating rink which opened in 1910 and closed in the early 1920s when it became a garage. The Ritz closed in 1961 and the town's telephone exchange was built on the site in 1970.

In 1912 Kate Marsden FRGS (1859-1932) and the Reverend J.C. Thompson FGS began to plan for a town museum. Kate Marsden was one of the first female Fellows of the Royal Geographical Society. In 1891 she had undertaken an expedition to Siberia in search of a cure for leprosy and later wrote of her adventures in the book *On Sledge and Horseback to the Outcast Siberian Lepers*. Kate Marsden had been the subject of scandal earlier in her life, the nature of which is now uncertain, but this appears to have been a closely guarded secret when she moved to Bexhill. She had amassed a large collection of tropical shells and Thompson had his own collection of geological specimens and their intention was to donate them to the borough when the new museum was opened. However, the council informed Marsden and Thompson that, if they wanted a museum, they must run it themselves. Bexhill Museum opened in 1914 in the Egerton Park Shelter Hall and Reverend Thompson was its first curator. The council provided the premises and a small grant, and it was agreed that the town mayor should be on the executive committee. Unfortunately the then mayor, Daniel Mayer, knew of Kate's secret and made it public by refusing to join the committee as long as she was associated with the museum. Not wishing to hinder the new organisation, Kate Marsden withdrew and later left Bexhill. Henry Sargent was appointed as assistant curator in 1920 and assumed the role of curator later that year, remaining in the post until his death in 1983.

114 *The Carter and Lidstone Garage in Western Road, c. 1922. The building was the Cinema de Luxe from 1913 until 1921. It was extended eastwards in 1923. On the left the corner of the Picture Playhouse is visible.*

115 *Kate Marsden preparing for her Siberian adventure in 1891.*

116 *Little Folks Home, Little Common, c.1913. This children's home opened in 1911.*

The First World War and Cooden Camp

The First World War arrived in Bexhill on 30 August 1914, when the band of the 15th Hussars was playing at the Colonnade; they cut short their performance and returned to barracks. The band of the Welsh Fusiliers, who were booked to play the following week, cancelled. The next day the local Territorials received their call-up papers. Many of Bexhill's hotels employed foreign staff to give an impression of continental elegance and as war approached they gave notice and returned to their own countries. This gave rise to rumours, probably unfounded, that they were German spies. The *Sackville Hotel* employed 20 German, Swiss and French staff; the manager is reported to have remarked, 'The war is killing the season'. Deutsches Paedagogium, the German school started by Mrs Du Mont, was closed and its headmaster

Dr Blassneck was interned. Because of their German background the Du Mont family left Bexhill at the start of the war. The town became home for 200 Belgian refugees after their country was invaded.

Cooden Camp military training area was established on Henry Young's property at Cooden Mount in 1914. Henry Young's tennis pavilion was converted into an army hospital and Belinda Cottages became a mess. At Cooden Camp, Lieutenant-Colonel Claude Lowther of Herstmonceux raised the 11th, 12th and 13th Battalions of the Royal Sussex Regiment, nicknamed 'Lowther's Lambs'. They stayed until the summer of 1915. On 15 August a company of the King's Royal Rifle Corp arrived and, with the remaining soldiers at the camp, formed the 14th Battalion of the Royal Sussex Regiment.

117 *Police commandeering a horse outside the* Castle Hotel, *1914. At the start of the First World War, horses and cars were commandeered by the military.*

118 *Soldiers at Cooden Camp, c.1914, take a break from working on a large pile of coal.*

119 *Cooden Camp, Princess Patricia Canadian Red Cross Hospital, c.1918. Cooden Camp was established on the land of Henry Young of Cooden Mount in 1914.*

Based at the camp in 1914 was Dr Walter Amsden, previously medical officer to the great Egyptologist Sir William Flinders Petrie, whom he had helped with his excavations. Amsden and his wife were friends of Kate Marsden, and she persuaded him to donate his Egyptology collection to the newly opened Bexhill Museum. At the start of September 1915 the South African Heavy Artillery arrived at Cooden Camp. With them was Major Nugent FitzPatrick who was killed at Beaumetz, France on 14 December 1917; it was his father Sir Percy FitzPatrick, who suggested to King George V that two minutes' silence be observed on the 11th hour of the 11th of November, the date the Armistice was signed.

The 'B' Siege Depot of the Royal Garrison Artillery came to the camp on 9 September and the 'A' Siege Depot on 15 November 1915; attached to them was a contingent of Australian Artillery. 'A' Depot departed on 25 July 1916 and 'B' Depot took over the camp and were renamed No.1 Reinforcing Depot Royal Siege Artillery. The South African Artillery left the camp later in 1916 and the rest of the Artillery finally departed on 9 January 1918. The Canadian Army Medical Corps arrived at Cooden Camp on 13 January 1918 and, with a party of Canadian Engineers, transformed it into the Princess Patricia Canadian Red Cross Hospital.

As well as the camp's military hospital, another was established in Cantelupe Road. Wounded soldiers helped to run the Bijou Cinema in Town Hall Square, for patriotic reasons renamed the St George's Cinema in 1917. The Kursaal was also renamed the Pavilion, after an outcry in the tabloid press that Bexhill had an entertainment venue with a German name. The people of Bexhill bought

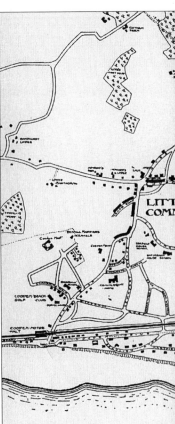

120 *Above: Peace declaration at the Town Hall, 2 July 1919.*

121 *Top right: Peace Day, Egerton Park, 19 July 1919.*

122 *Right: 1925 Map of Bexhill.*

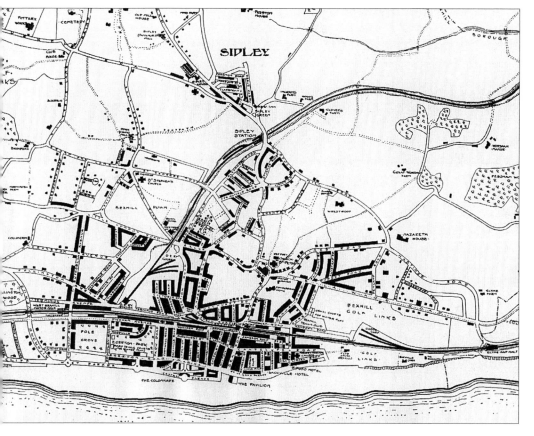

123 *The War Memorial on the seafront, c.1925. This was opened on 12 December 1920. In the background to the left of the memorial is Marina Garage, and to the right is the* Wilton Court Hotel, *which was built in 1900.*

so many War Bonds during the First World War that the town was later given an army tank, which stood for many years on the sea front as recognition of local patriotism.

The 5th Battalion of the Royal Sussex Regiment had been quartered in the French village of Bayencourt in 1916; it was to be devastated during the war. In 1923 the Mayor of Bexhill, Councillor E.W.C. Bowrey, initiated a project to adopt and support Bayencourt. Bexhill provided for a water tower and piped water supply for the village and Bowrey led a civic delegation to Bayencourt in 1924. Further support was given and another visit was made in 1930. The connection is commemorated by the Bexhill street names of Bayencourt North and Bayencourt South.

A huge crowd gathered to hear the reading of the peace declaration outside the Town Hall on 2 July 1919 and a thanksgiving service was held in the Egerton Park Pergola on 6 July. The celebrations continued with Peace Day processions around Bexhill on 19 July and for Demobilised Men's Day on 10 September 1919.

The war had claimed many local lives which were commemorated through the town's war memorials. The first was a Peace Memorial outside St Mary Magdalene's church, designed by the Mayor, George Herbert Gray, and unveiled on 2 November 1919. The Little Common War Memorial was unveiled on 21 November 1920, and Brigadier-General H. O'Donnell unveiled the War Memorial on Bexhill's sea front on 12 December 1920.

In 1914 the 8th Earl De La Warr was again in trouble. His second wife divorced him on the grounds of adultery and desertion and his creditors were pursuing him through the courts. At the start of the First World War he bought a commission and left the country. He was first a major in the Southdown Battalion of the Royal Sussex Regiment and then joined the Royal Naval Volunteer Reserves, being given command of the motor cruiser *Nord Est*. Unfortunately the Earl contracted fever and died in Messina on 16 December 1915. Muriel, Lady De La Warr became lady of the manor of Bexhill until her son Herbrand assumed the lordship in 1921.

Seven

THE 9TH EARL AND THE
DE LA WARR PAVILION

Herbrand Edward Dundonald Brassey Sackville, the 9th Earl De La Warr, or 'Buck' as he was also known, was the most charismatic leader the town has ever had. As Mayor of Bexhill from 1932-5 he championed the building of a new entertainment pavilion for the use of the townspeople and to draw in holidaymakers. He was a remarkable man, the first hereditary peer to represent the Labour Party and Bexhill's first socialist mayor.

The 9th Earl's mother Lady De La Warr, née Brassey, was the greatest influence on him. As a child she had sailed around the world with her family and encountered many different cultures. The Brasseys were Liberal. Her father Earl Brassey, had been Liberal MP for Hastings, and Gladstone would stay with the family at their home, Normanhurst Court in Catsfield, with his entire cabinet. Muriel was actively involved with the fight for women's suffrage before the First World War and because of this she joined the Labour Party. She was a close friend of the Labour MP George Lansbury and of Annie Besant, the President of the Theosophical Society. Muriel herself became a Theosophist, and when in 1911 Annie Besant brought to England Krishnamurti, the young Indian boy who they believed to be the new Messiah, he lived for much of his stay with Muriel and her children. The political and spiritual views of his mother stayed with the

124   *The 9th Earl De La Warr as Mayor of Bexhill, 1932.*

9th Earl and he became a socialist, vegetarian and a pacifist. Although unwilling to take life, he did wish to serve his country and, aged 16, served on a minesweeper during the First World War.

It is usually considered that the history of the Pavilion started in 1933 when the 9th Earl proposed a scheme for a new £50,000 entertainment pavilion in Bexhill. Its background

95

125 *Players in the Bexhill Pageant of 20 July 1927 outside the British Legion Club in London Road.*

goes back much further than this, however, since before the First World War there had been demand for a better entertainment venue in Bexhill. The Earl's achievement was to bring it to fruition; many had tried before but it took his energy and diplomatic skills to make it a reality.

The 9th Earl created the *Cooden Beach Hotel* in 1931 by converting a row of buildings on the site. Located next to Cooden Beach railway station, the hotel served the Cooden Beach Golf Club, which was constructed by the 8th Earl in 1912.

In May 1933 Princess Helena Victoria opened the new Bexhill Hospital, attended by the 9th Earl in his capacity as mayor. There had been demand for a hospital since before the First World War and 'Hospital Demonstrations' were held by the local friendly societies to petition for one. Another of the high points of 1933 was a visit to Little Common by Sir Alan Cobham's Flying Circus; the Earl and his family joined the crowds of people who took advantage of the opportunity to see the town from the air.

As well as the De La Warr Pavilion the presence of Arthur Spray, made famous through the book about him called *The Mysterious Cobbler*, made Bexhill well known in the 1930s. Spray lived and worked at 16 Station Road, and was a cobbler renowned for his powers as a healer.

126 *Bexhill Orient Football Club, 1923-4.*

127 *Bexhill Hospital, c.1935. The hospital, situated on Holliers Hill, opened in May 1933.*

128 *Waghorn's Garage, at the junction of Buckhurst and Station Roads, 1929. The site is still a filling station.*

129 *Cornford & Spray's cobblers shop, 18 Station Road, c.1930. On the left is Arthur Spray, 'The Mysterious Cobbler', so-called because of his healing powers, and next to him is Jim Cornford.*

As with any community there have always been divisions within Bexhill. Sometimes these splits acted as a catalyst and stimulated the town's development, and at others they held it back by needless argument. The first main division was between the areas of the town owned by the De La Warr estate, and those which were not. The sea front was divided in two by Sea Road which, south of the railway line, defined the boundary of the Webb estate to the west and the De La Warr estate to the east. There were also social divisions. Trade and tradesmen were viewed as necessary evils by the upper strata of society, useful, but never to be mixed with socially. However, many of the traders were also suspicious of the De La Warr estate's influence in town politics. The commercial infrastructure of the town was located in Webb's territory, which was known as the Egerton Park estate, and the high-class housing, hotels and entertainment venues were mostly on the De La Warr estate.

A more damaging division was of trades-men and hoteliers versus residents. This was unconnected to the split between the Webb and De La Warr estates. It was really a conflict between those dependent on tourism for their livelihood and those who were not. Residents living on independent means seemed to find visitors to the resort an intrusion, and resent-ed tradesmen who gave them preferential treatment. More importantly, these residents were not prepared to pay higher rates for facilities to attract visitors to Bexhill, or for their entertainment.

At the heart of most, if not all, of the arguments within Bexhill were the rates; an-ything that would cost the resident ratepayers money was viewed with the deepest suspicion. Tourism, of course, was as important for the shopkeepers and publicans on Webb's estate as it was for the hoteliers on De La Warr Parade; they were both dependent on rich visitors coming to Bexhill and spending freely.

In the early days of the resort entertainment on the sea front was based around two focal points, the Kursaal on De La Warr Parade and the Colonnade by the coastguard station on the Horn. The cartoons of the period clearly show the social divisions between the two venues: the Kursaal for the upper-middle classes and above, and the Colonnade for the lower-middle classes and below. Development of Central Parade began in 1909 and culmi-nated with the opening of the Colonnade in 1911. This was not free from controversy and a cartoon in the Christmas 1909 edition of the *Bexhill Observer* portrayed bands from the Kursaal and Colonnade trying to drown out each other and scaring away all the town's visitors in the process.

From 1907 various proposals were made for a 'Winter Garden' or some form of large enclosed entertainments pavilion. Proposed sites included the Kursaal, the Colonnade and Egerton Park. The roller-skating rink in Buckhurst Road was briefly used as a winter garden in 1921, before it was converted into a garage and later replaced by a cinema.

The Kursaal's popularity began to decline after 1907 and the 8th Earl sold it to Mr Claude Johnson in 1908; it was said that the Earl had lost some £30,000 over the building. In 1912 and 1913 more cartoons appeared in the local newspapers showing a winter garden on the sea front and the rivalry between the Kursaal and Colonnade, both of which wanted to be the site of the new pavilion. The Kursaal's management even proposed completing their premises as a pier, by building on to it the Winter Garden and a new theatre out over the sea. The Kursaal was substantially and unflatteringly modified in 1925 and in its last years produced Bexhill's first repertory company, Philip York's Country Players, who began performances in 1932.

In 1913 the Bexhill Corporation finally bought De La Warr Parade. The De La Warr Gates had enabled the 8th Earl to close off the sea front symbolically, allowing him to control the provision of entertainment on his estate. Shortly after the Corporation acquired the land they demolished the De La Warr Gates, removing a powerful reminder of the Earl's authority in Bexhill. The only portion of the sea front still in private hands was the site of the Kursaal. An unsuccessful attempt was made to purchase the land in 1927, but eight years later, in October 1935, a deal was completed and the Kursaal was demolished, leaving the entire sea front in public ownership.

The Corporations Act of 1923 permitted increased expenditure by local councils on public buildings for entertainment and so paved

130 'The Magical Machine', Bexhill Observer *cartoon, 1910, possibly depicting the then mayor Alderman J.A. Paton. Concern over the rates has always been central to the politics of the town.*

131 'The Parting of the Ways', *1913. A cartoon showing the audience for the Kursaal and the Colonnade. The Kursaal was more up-market and largely for visitors to the resort; the Colonnade was the centre of entertainment for residents.*

132 'Everybody's wanting it', Bexhill Observer *cartoon, 1913. There was competition between the Kursaal and the Colonnade to become the site of the proposed Winter Garden Pavilion, later realised in 1935 as the De La Warr Pavilion.*

133   *Kursaal and 'Dodgems', 1933. The site now occupied by the Sailing Club was once an entertainment area; the Kursaal was a theatre and the 'Dodgems' offered traditional seaside entertainment.*

the way for greater municipal development in Bexhill. The Corporation commissioned the consultants Adams, Thompson & Fry to produce a development plan for the town in 1926. A preliminary report was returned in 1927 and the final version was published in 1930 as the Bexhill Borough General Development Plan. It advocated a radical redevelopment of the whole borough. If implemented, this ambitious scheme would have demolished most of the town and rebuilt it in 1930s style. It included a proposal for a 'Music Pavilion and Enlarged Band Enclosure' on the Colonnade site. It also contained a bold plan to redevelop

Town Hall Square, including a new railway station and a link between the Crowhurst branch line and the main south coast railway line. Needless to say, the recommendations of the Development Plan were not implemented; however it seems to have tipped the balance in favour of the Colonnade rather than the Kursaal site for the future construction of the De La Warr Pavilion.

As mayor, Councillor A. Turner Laing outlined his plan for a new pavilion on the site of the coastguard station, behind the Colonnade, in January 1930. The firm of Tubbs and Messer drew up the plans

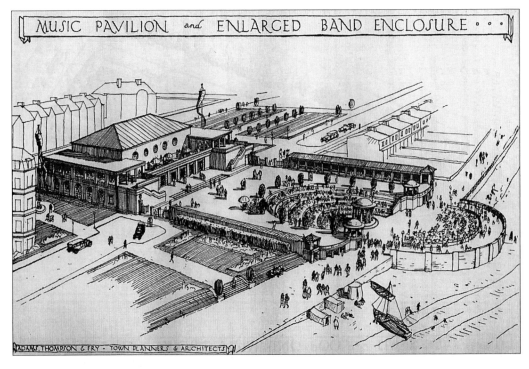

MUSIC PAVILION and ENLARGED BAND ENCLOSURE · · ·

ADAMS, THOMPSON & FRY · TOWN PLANNERS & ARCHITECTS

134 *Adams, Thompson & Fry's 1930 development plan proposal for a music pavilion and bandstand at the Colonnade site. This was never built but it was the first time a modern-style building was suggested for the sea front, something that was finally achieved in 1935 with the opening of the De La Warr Pavilion.*

and the £50,000 scheme outlined an entertainments hall complex, which included a museum, library and reading room, but the long-standing disagreement between those who wanted to promote Bexhill as a resort and those who wanted it to be entirely residential prevented the plan from being implemented at this time.

So it was that in April 1933 the 9th Earl De La Warr, as mayor of Bexhill, proposed a new £50,000 plan for an entertainment hall on the coastguard site. Through shrewd politics and public consultation the project had overwhelming support, something that was almost unheard of in the town. The coastguard station closed in August 1930 leaving the

land free for development. The 9th Earl De La Warr commented, 'We all of us want to maintain the existing character of the town, but we believe that we can make more of our existing resources.' He was determined that the project should be funded by the town and not be a private development and said, 'My own view is if it is going to pay private enterprise it is going to pay the town.'

It was decided to ask the RIBA to hold a competition to design the new building and president Sir Raymond Unwin selected as judge Thomas S. Tait, who was respected by the establishment but was known to be sympathetic towards the ideals of new 'modernist' architects.

Bexhill Borough Council prepared a tight brief, indicating that a building in the modern style was wanted and that 'heavy stonework is not desirable'. The competition was announced in *The Architects Journal* of 7 September 1933 and the closing date was 4 December 1933. Two hundred and thirty designs were submitted. The results of the competition were announced in *The Architects Journal* of 8 February 1934 and the designs displayed at the York Hall in London Road from 6 to 13 February 1934. So that the designs could be judged on their own merits, the names of the architects were not revealed until the judging had finished. Erich Mendelsohn and Serge Chermayeff won the £150 first prize, Tait commenting that their design 'indicated a thorough grasp of the nature of the problem, is direct and simple in planning, and

shows a masterly handling of the architectural treatment'. Of the proposed entertainment hall he went on to say, 'This is the only scheme submitted showing a satisfactory treatment in this respect'. The design was the clear winner and the correspondent for *The Architects Journal* commented, 'Mr Thomas S. Tait must have had little difficulty in choosing the winner'. The only early objections to the result were from British Fascists and one Bexhill resident who was opposed to 'alien architects' working in this country.

The submitted design was slightly different from the one that was used; the two minor criticisms that Tait made of it were worked into the final version. The scheme was to redevelop the Colonnade site completely and to link it with the main building. In July 1935 the council proposed to incorporate a

135 *The original architect's model of the De La Warr Pavilion, 1934, made to secure a loan to build it. The model shows the full extent of the project, with a seafront swimming pool linked to the main building by an enclosed walkway, a pier with diving board and a large statue. The model is now in the collection of Bexhill Museum.*

swimming pool in the redeveloped Colonnade, from which there also extended a small pier and diving board.

The budget for the project was £50,000, but Mendelsohn and Chermayeff estimated the cost of their initial design at £58,260. At a meeting on 19 February 1934 it was decided to apply to the Ministry of Health for a loan of £80,000 to cover the project. To secure the loan a Public Inquiry was needed, and this was held on two days from 5 April 1934, when the large architect's model, which is still exhibited at Bexhill Museum, was first displayed. On 28 September 1934 permission was given for a loan of £70,000 to be repaid over 30 years and an additional £8,412 to be repaid over 15 years.

The spectre of ratepayers' money being spent ignited opposition to the project and a residents' association was formed to oppose the building of the Pavilion. Hostility over the nationality of the architects or the aesthetics of their design took second place to the underlying fear of the council spending public money on a facility for the use of visitors. At a council meeting on 28 October 1935 the decision to delay the £18,600 swimming pool at the Colonnade was made, and on 19 November 1935 the plans for the £8,734 redesign of the Colonnade and the linking pergola were

136 *'That Statue Business'*, Bexhill Independent *cartoon, 1935. The newspaper was opposed to the idea of a statue and swimming pool as part of the De La Warr Pavilion complex. It points out that much of the concern was over the cost of the project rather than the aesthetics of the finished statue.*

137 *Building the De La Warr Pavilion, May 1935. The view across the restaurant roof has Marina Court in the background. The welded steel frame of the building is clearly shown.*

deferred. Neither scheme ever materialised. Early photographs of the Pavilion show that part of the pergola adjoining the main building was constructed but was subsequently removed. A huge statue by Frank Dobson was intended to stand on the south terrace of the Pavilion but, although a maquette was exhibited, the piece was never installed.

The contract stated that the building work should be completed in fifty weeks and as much local labour as possible should

be employed on the project. Construction began in January 1935. During March, King George V and Queen Mary visited the 9th Earl at Cooden Beach, and expressed an interest in the model of the Pavilion which was shown to them. They were so intrigued that they then made an unscheduled visit to the building site. A commemorative plaque was laid by the 9th Earl De La Warr on 6 May 1935, the Silver Jubilee day of George V, when he said:

In doing so I mark a great day in the history of Bexhill, for which we have rightly chosen a great day in the history of our nation. How better could we dedicate ourselves today than by gathering round this new venture of ours, a venture which is going to lead to the growth, the prosperity and the greater culture of this, our town; a venture also which is part of a great national movement virtually to found a new industry – the industry of giving that relaxation, that pleasure, that culture, which hitherto the gloom and dreariness of British resorts has driven our fellow country men to seek in foreign lands. It is the expression of our determination to make a town, and therefore a body of citizens, of which His Gracious Majesty King George V, even in this his jubilee, may be justly proud.

The De La Warr Pavilion was opened by the Duke and Duchess of York on 12 December 1935. They were presented with a bouquet by Lady Kitty Sackville, daughter of the 9th Earl, who had agreed to do so only if she were accompanied by her friend Captain Jim Stevens of the Bexhill Fire Brigade. The two had become close friends when the brigade had named their fire engine after her. It is said that the Duchess of York caught a cold during the visit and vowed never to return to Bexhill.

The correspondent for the *New Statesman* of 1936 commented:

You could not find a stronger argument in favour of town planning than Bexhill, which is not so much a town as a chaotic litter of hideous houses sprawling higgledy piggledy along a lovely coast. Lord De La Warr, whose ancestors were responsible for this muddle, has now made an act of reparation. The most satisfactory example of modern architecture I have seen in this country ... One has the impression of being on a great transatlantic liner. The Functionalists can complain that the staircase on the North side is mere ornament and its great glass bay looks only on buildings better not looked at - but it is a good ornament. The traditionalist on the other hand will complain that this is not

138 *The De La Warr Pavilion, c.1950. The* Metropole Hotel *is in the background.*

so much a pleasure pavilion as a pleasure machine, ominously appropriate to the standard amusements of Mr Huxley's Brave New World.

Bernard Shaw wrote, 'Delighted to hear that Bexhill has emerged from barbarism at last, but I shall not give it a clean bill of health until all my plays are performed there once a year at least!'

Shaw later attended a performance of his play *The Millionairess* at the De La Warr Pavilion in November 1936 and afterwards went backstage to speak to the cast.

139 *Johannes Schreiner's 1944 proposal for the addition of a dance hall to the east end of the De La Warr Pavilion.*

The Bexhill Corporation offered the 9th Earl the Freedom of the Borough in June 1936 but he turned it down, saying:

> I still feel it would be wiser for the matter to be deferred. It would naturally be pleasing to receive such an honour, feeling that it was with the approval of the Burgesses of Bexhill, but whilst so much controversy about the pavilion still exists, there would evidently be a certain number who would once again condemn the action of the council. I should naturally have been very proud and happy to receive such an honour, and you will easily understand that it is with grief and disappointment that I have come to this decision, but in the circumstances feel confident that I am adopting the only course possible.

The building suffered bomb damage during the Second World War and Johannes Schreiner wrote a Dilapidation Report in 1944. Schreiner had been Mendelsohn's assistant during the original work on the Pavilion and he presented plans for building a dance hall on the east end of the building and an extension from the theatre

on the south side, neither of which were implemented.

Various unflattering modifications were made to the building in the 1950s and there was even an attempt to hide the building under ivy in the 1970s. Restoration work during the 1990s has made the building structurally sound and in 2004 the next stage of improvements is about to start. This will restore the De La Warr Pavilion's role within Bexhill.

The Pavilion is not Bexhill's only claim to fame but it is certainly the best known; the national and international significance of the building cannot be doubted. It was controversial when it was first built and the controversy has not diminished. By constructing the De La Warr Pavilion in 1935, Bexhill showed itself to be progressive and forward thinking and has never quite recovered from the shock. It is still startling to see such a radically different architectural design within a town of mostly Victorian buildings.

Eight

THE SECOND WORLD WAR
TO THE PRESENT

The De La Warr Pavilion had lifted Bexhill's profile and re-invigorated the resort but the effect was to be short-lived, eclipsed as it was by the Second World War. Erich Mendelsohn, who with Russian-born Serge Chermayeff had designed the De La Warr Pavilion, was Jewish and had fled Nazi Germany in 1933, bringing the International Modernist style of architecture with him.

There are rumours that high-ranking German officials were seen at the *Cooden Beach Hotel* shortly before the start of the war; this might be true, although rather than planning an invasion they were probably here for the same reason as many other visitors to the town, to see their children who were at school here. The Augusta Victoria College in Dorset Road was a school for German girls to improve their English, and had the distinction of being the only Bexhill school with a badge which included the swastika. Von Ribbentrop's daughter and Himmler's goddaughter attended the Augusta Victoria College, which closed in 1939.

Gas masks were issued to the population in 1938 and some temporary air-raid shelters were built. Most schools continued through 1939, although precautions such as the addition of air-raid shelters for the staff and pupils were taken. This part of the south coast was considered to be safe and children from Lon-

don were evacuated here for their protection, 540 junior school pupils and 178 secondary school pupils coming to the town. While France stood between England and Germany there was no immediate invasion threat and life continued much as normal. Preparations such as the building of public air-raid shelters, the filling of sand bags on the beach and the presence of London schoolchildren were the only visible sign of activity during the 'Phoney War' period.

In 1940, following the fall of France, Bexhill was again under threat of invasion. The local children were evacuated in July 1940, St Barnabas' boys, St Barnabas' girls, St Peter's boys, St Mark's and St Mary Magdalene's school pupils all being sent to Letchworth, and St Peter's infants and Sidley infants being sent to Stevenage. A total of 1,120 children left Bexhill but many, despite the risks, were so unhappy that they returned home. By the end of 1940 about 350 were back and in January 1941 St Barnabas' boys, All Saints and St Mark's schools had to be reopened.

The Second World War is one of the periods of the town's history that we know least about. There was a high level of security, large portions of the population were absent and rumours were more plentiful than facts.

'At 4.30, June 2nd, 1940, on a summer's day all mare's tails and blue sky we

140 *Gas mask test in the Town Hall, 1938.*

141 *The Park Pavilion Café, Egerton Park, 1939. The building was a combined theatre and indoor bowling centre. During the Second World War it was used as a café offering 'a good meal for 4d'.*

142 *The Home Guard, Bexhill Down, August 1940. Inspection by Zone Commander C.H. Madden MC.*

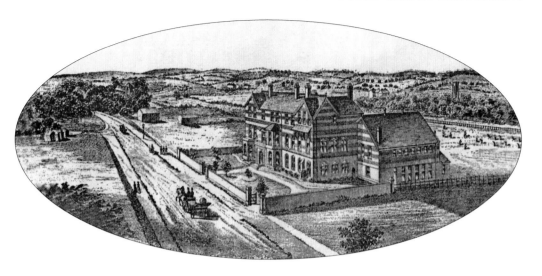

143 *Holmwood College, Hastings Road, c.1895. It later became Worthingholm School. Spike Milligan, as part of D Battery 56th Regiment Royal Artillery, was based here during the first part of the Second World War.*

arrived at Bexhill-on-Sea, where I got off. It wasn't easy. The train didn't stop there.'[1] This is how Spike Milligan described his introduction to Bexhill. He was stationed in Bexhill from June 1940 until February 1941 and recalls his time here in *Adolf Hitler: My Part In His Downfall.* As part of D Battery 56th Regiment Royal Artillery, Spike was based at Worthingholm School (formerly Holmwood) in Hastings Road and was often deployed at the observation post on top of Galley Hill. Another location mentioned is the W.V.S. Forces Corner, on the northern junction of Sea Road and Cantelupe Road. Formerly the popular café, Sydenham House, which opened in 1897, this was given over to military use during the war. Writing for the *Goon Show* in 1954, Spike Milligan immortalised the town in the episode entitled 'The Dreaded Batter Pudding Hurler (of Bexhill-on-Sea)', which was set in 1941.

The beach was closed off by a wall of barbed wire along the edge of the promenade, concrete tank-traps blocked obvious landing places and some areas were mined. There are also rumours of incendiary devices located on the foreshore but this has not been proved. Light anti-aircraft guns were installed around the town in 1941, later to be supported by armoured cars with machine guns in 1942, and heavy anti-aircraft guns were placed on the Promenade in 1944.

Following the Battle of Britain the threat of invasion was reduced, but air raids and tip-and-run strikes were still regular occurrences. In total there were 51 air raids on Bexhill, 2,735 buildings were lightly damaged, 189 seriously damaged and 21 buildings totally destroyed. About 328 high explosive bombs fell on Bexhill besides thousands of incendi-aries. German fighters and the gunners on bombers strafed the streets with machine-gun fire, and towards the end of the war there were

144   *Demolition of the Crowhurst viaduct, 1969.*

flying bomb attacks. There were 21 civilian deaths and one soldier was killed. Most of the residential housing that was damaged or destroyed was repaired or rebuilt after the war but the effects of the bombing can still be seen in Devonshire Road, where occasional low-rise blocks of shops fill the gaps between the taller elegant Victorian buildings.

One of the most intriguing stories involving Bexhill in the Second World War is the alleged visit of Winston Churchill to the town in 1944. He was staying at Normanhurst Court, in Catsfield, and passed through on his way to Hastings. While here he attended an important meeting at 'the hut', a structure

that had once been the chapel of the Beehive School in Dorset Road. Here it is said he discussed plans for the Normandy landings with his generals.

John Logie Baird arrived in Bexhill in 1941; he lived in a large house at the junction of Station Road and Sea Road, now known as Baird Court. Baird had become famous after making the first successful demonstration of television in Hastings in 1924. Although his design for television was not the one that became standard it was the first. He suffered from poor health and his choice of Bexhill may have been due to its suitability as a place to convalesce. He continued to invent while in Bexhill and was planning to demonstrate a new television system when the war ended, but his health deteriorated and he died of pneumonia in 1946.

Many of the independent schools did not return to Bexhill after the war and those that did gradually declined. It was probably the end of the British Empire's colonies, and in particular the independence of India in 1947, which finished off the schools as many of the pupils had been left as boarders in Bexhill by parents working overseas. As people returned to England many relocated to Bexhill; they had discovered the town when they or their children had been educated here, although others would have been advised by their doctors to relocate to Bexhill for its therapeutic qualities. The post-war town acquired a reputation for being inhabited by 'gouty colonels' and 'old colonials', who had not fully adjusted to life in England and were attempting to continue their former lifestyle. The replacement of schools by residential housing did not benefit the local economy. Many of those who moved to Bexhill were retired and living on fixed incomes so had to be cautious in their spending. The proportion of the residents of independent means began to outnumber those who worked in the tourist economy and so it became politically more difficult to spend ratepayers' money on facilities for visitors. Gradually the town lost its way as a resort and became more residential in character.

In 1964 the Crowhurst branch line closed. As a result Bexhill lost its fast rail link to London and Bexhill West and Sidley stations became redundant. The Down Arch, which carried the line over the A259, was demolished in 1967 and the Crowhurst Viaduct was blown up in 1969, ending any hope that

the line could ever be reopened. The closure of the Polegate rail link, which bypassed Eastbourne on the Victoria line and saved about 20 minutes on the journey to London, led to the increasing isolation of Bexhill. The only reminder of the Crowhurst line is the name of the light industrial site built on land south of the A259, through which runs Beeching Road, named after the man responsible for the line's closure.

The decline of Bexhill as a seaside resort can best be seen through the loss of the town's larger hotels. The *Marine Hotel*, built at the seaward end of Devonshire Road in 1895, was purchased by successful London draper John Reynolds Roberts, who turned it into Roberts Marine Mansions, a holiday home for drapers. Second World War bombing damaged the building and it was demolished in 1954. Dalmore Court was built on the site in 1961. The *Metropole Hotel* also suffered from bomb damage and the effects of a serious fire when used as an RAF billet; it was finally demolished in 1955, after standing derelict from the end of the war. The *Sackville Hotel* closed in 1960, although the building survives despite an attempt to clear and develop the site in 1962. Only the *Granville Hotel*, later named the *Grand Hotel*, was to survive until 2000, when it was abandoned as a commercial enterprise. In 2003, much of the building was severely damaged by fire and demolished for safety reasons. The loss of the last of the great town-centre hotels is a poignant one. The *Cooden Beach Hotel* has continued to provide accommodation and is still an elegant venue.

Bexhill Corporation commissioned a short promotional film which captured the highlights of the summer season of 1960. By then relatively cheap package holidays had become available and Bexhill was no longer competing for visitors only with other British seaside towns but also with foreign resorts that could virtually guarantee fine weather. Lasting for just over a quarter of an hour, it would have played at cinemas before a main feature to attract visitors to Bexhill. It is significant that the last few minutes of the film are about relocating to Bexhill and not just visiting, as if admitting that it was no longer wholly a resort.

Queen Elizabeth II and the Duke of Edinburgh honoured Bexhill with a royal visit in 1966. Despite appalling weather a civic reception was held at the De La Warr Pavilion. The Queen's next appointment was at the devastated Welsh village of Aberfan and Bexhill nurses raised disaster relief funds during the royal visit.

The most radical proposal for redesigning Bexhill was put forward in 1967. The Bexhill Corporation commissioned a development plan in 1962 from the firm of Stillman and Eastwick-Field, who published their report in January 1967. They recommended the demolition and rebuilding of central Bexhill with high-rise blocks made of cast concrete, the whole scheme to be completed by 1986. A multi-storey car park and office block was to be constructed over the railway line, to link Station Road with Devonshire Square, a plan that was to be proposed again and once more rejected in the 1970s. Had the 1960s development plan been implemented, much of Bexhill would now be unrecognisable, and on the seafront the De La Warr Pavilion would be the oldest building rather than the youngest. Like the 1930 development plan, it addressed many of the problems that still concern residents, such as the road layout and car parking.

The appearance of the sea front was transformed in 1970 when the huge apartment block, Marina Court, was demolished. The 'triangular plot' was again available and became an extension of the De La Warr Pavilion car park. The *Metropole Hotel* and Marina Court both had shops at street level, extending the town centre's retail area onto Marina. With both buildings gone, the De La Warr Pavilion was left as the only large structure on the sea front.

Out to sea, the southern horizon acquired a new feature in June 1971, when the Royal Sovereign Light Tower was floated out from Newhaven, where it was built, and positioned on the Royal Sovereign Reef. This replaced the Royal Sovereign Lightship, which warned sailors of the presence of the reef from 1875. The Light Tower became fully automated and the crew were removed on 13 May 1994.

A new Bexhill landmark was to appear in 1972. The buildings in Collington Avenue that had been St John's School from 1910 and, from 1947, the Royal Merchant Navy School, were demolished and replaced by Thrift House in 1972-3. This high-rise office block was built for the Hastings and Thanet Building Society, and is now known as Conquest House, headquarters of Hastings Direct Insurance. Because of the size of the building, set in what is otherwise residential area, and the additional height of the aerial masts bristling above it, it is the major landmark of western Bexhill. Another striking feature on Bexhill's skyline was lost when the Metropolitan Convalescent Home, on the brow of Bexhill Hill, was demolished in 1988.

West Parade developed very slowly. The Victorian development ended with Marine Crescent, opposite the putting green by the De La Warr Pavilion. Except for the elegant

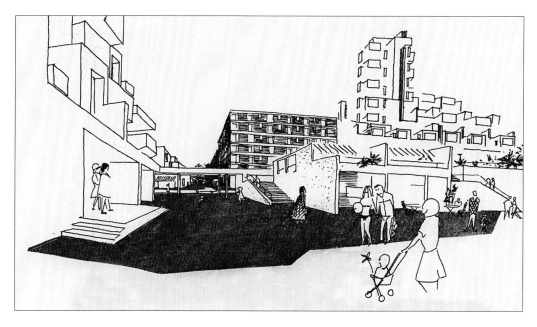

145 *Concept sketch from Bexhill's 1967 development plan. Produced by the firm of Stillman and Eastwick-Field for the Bexhill Corporation, it proposed to demolish most of the town centre and rebuild it in cast concrete.*

house Oceania, which was built in 1903, most of the development is post-war. It is now dominated by the six large apartment blocks known as the 'West Indies' because each is named after a West Indian island. Construction began in the late 1960s and was completed by March 1978. Prior to this there had been some discussion about building a yachting marina on this site.

The most serious loss to Bexhill's heritage occurred when the Manor House was demolished in 1968. This was done largely because of the need to widen the road through the Old Town, still at that time the main road to Hastings and very constricted at that point. Controversy arose over a proposal to build an apartment block of several storeys on the site overshadowing the old village. The Old Town Preservation Society was formed and the plan rejected. The Manor Gardens were created on the site and the lower walls of part of the Manor House were retained as ornamental features. Princess Alexandra officially opened the Manor Gardens in 1972, as part of the celebrations for the 1,200th anniversary of the King Offa Charter. The anniversary year was the last great civic occasion for the Bexhill Corporation as it was succeeded by Rother District Council in 1974.

More of Bexhill's history was lost to road building when work began on the Old Town bypass in 1978; known as King Offa Way, it opened in 1980. To enable its construction, the settlement at the lower part of Belle Hill was demolished, including the *Queen's Head*, which dated back to the days of the King's German Legion.

146 *Bexhill Old Town, c.1955. This shows the key buildings in the original Bexhill village, the Manor House,* *the* Bell Hotel *and St Peter's church, catering for the administrative, social and spiritual needs of the community.*

Most of the buildings facing the Town Hall in Buckhurst Place were demolished in 1974 and work began on a new branch of Sainsbury's supermarket, which opened in 1976 replacing the store formerly in Devonshire Road.

The Egerton Park swimming pool was demolished in 1987. This had been modernised in the 1960s and '70s but was closed in the middle of the '80s when the pool cracked and could not be repaired. A replacement swimming pool was part of a package negotiated by

Rother District Council for the commercial development of the former Hastings Gasworks site at Glyne Gap.

In 1974 Bexhill Corporation ceased to exist when Rother District Council was created. Bexhill Town Hall became the headquarters of the new local authority, serving Bexhill, Battle, Winchelsea, Rye and the rural areas around Hastings. Whereas the other towns retained their town councils, Bexhill did not. However, the royal charter of 1902 had given Bexhill the right to appoint a mayor, an office that could not be dispensed with and was renamed the Charter Mayor; this honorary position within the town was funded via the Bexhill Precept on the Council Tax. Charter Mayors are chosen from Bexhill councillors and when their term of office ends they become Charter Trustees. Their main function is to elect the new Charter Mayor and preserve the town plate, insignia and civic ceremonial.

Rother District Council developed the Ravenside superstores and leisure complex at Glyne Gap, which was built in 1989 on the site of the Hastings Gasworks demolished in 1971. The out-of-town retail park drew custom away from the town centre, leaving many premises empty or occupied by charity shops.

The situation has improved recently and there is a successful scheme for the refurbishment of shop frontages. One of the unique features of Bexhill's town centre is that it is still made up largely of independent shops rather than retail chains and has avoided the fate of many towns, an anonymous high street with the same shops stocking the same goods. The character of the town is still alive and well. At the end of 2003 work began on the much needed redevelopment of Devonshire Square, which will provide a useful public space within the town centre.

Bexhill's motoring connections were not restricted to the start of the 20th century. In 1954 the Jubilee Speed Trials were held, renewing interest in the town's racing history.

147 *Hastings gasworks, Glyne Gap, Bexhill, c.1960. Watercolour by Edwin Keen. Ravenside superstores and leisure complex was built on the site in 1989.*

148 *Elva Courier, c.1960.*

This was the first event to feature veteran cars rather than current models. Local enthusiasts revived the tradition again in 1990, by organising the first 'Bexhill 100 Festival of Motoring'. This key feature culminated in the final event of 2002, which celebrated the 100th anniversary of Britain's first motor car race, here in Bexhill.

The town is also the birthplace of the Elva car. Frank Nichols, its inventor, who was born in Bexhill in 1920, first opened a small garage in Pevensey in the late 1940s but later set up a garage in London Road, Bexhill, where he produced the first Elva car. Unable to expand his premises in Bexhill, he moved the business to Rye in 1961. Production ceased in 1969.

Bexhill's association with motor sports was revived in 1993 when students at St Richard's Catholic College set a new land speed record for an electrically powered car of its class with Project Volta. Volta achieved a speed of 106.748 m.p.h. and was the result of two years' work by a team of four students led by their teacher Peter Fairhurst.

There are many fascinating characters associated with Bexhill in the post-war period. The actor Desmond Llewelyn (1914-99) moved to Bexhill Old Town in 1965. He became a well loved and much respected member of the community and was a vice-president of the Old Town Preservation Society. He was best known as 'Q' in the James Bond films.

Alex Sanders, self-styled 'King of the Witches', moved to Chantry Cottage in Bexhill Old Town in 1973. He was born in Lancashire in 1926 and, aged seven, was initiated into witchcraft by his grandmother. Aliester Crowley, 'The Great Beast' who spent his last years in Hastings and died there in 1947, marked him with a magical symbol at the age of ten. Alex Sanders was credited with the leadership of 107 'Alexandrian' covens worldwide.[2] His Bexhill coven held meetings at Chantry Cottage as well as the De La Warr Pavilion, the Manor Gardens and, possibly for refreshment, the *Bell Hotel*. Sanders famously put a curse on a Bexhill Light Opera and Dramatic Society's production at the De La Warr Pavilion, following an argument between his wife, Gillian, who was the musical director and the producer. Later it was said the 'curse' had been meant as a joke. Whatever the truth, it gave the BLODS the best publicity they ever had, with stories appearing in the national press and the producer being interviewed on local radio. Towards the end of his life, in 1986, Sanders moved to St Leonards, where he died aged 62 in 1988. During the 1970s Bexhill was also the home to an organisation calling itself the 'World Institute of Occult Sciences' based in Albert Road.[3]

Bexhill's most famous son is the actor and stand-up comedian Eddie Izzard. Eddie was born in Aden in 1962. His family had lived in Sidley for generations, his grandmother helping to found the Sidley Community

149 *Sidley Community Association playgroup, Sidley House in the 1950s. At the back of the room on the left is Mrs Izzard and on the right Mrs Rummary.*

150   *Collington Wood, c.1930.*

Association in 1949. Eddie came to Bexhill briefly in 1962 and stayed for a year from 1963-4. After living in Northern Ireland and South Wales he returned to Bexhill in 1969 and was educated in Eastbourne where he acquired his love of acting. He worked in his youth selling ice creams in a kiosk at the foot of Galley Hill and at the restaurant in the De La Warr Pavilion.

The Great Storm of 1987 struck on the night of 15-16 October and left a trail of destruction across the country; Bexhill was subjected to sustained wind speeds of 85 to 96m.p.h. which caused substantial damage to homes and businesses. Boats were left stranded halfway up Sackville Road and Collington Wood was levelled. Rising sea levels and climate change mean the town is still very much at the mercy of the elements.

Regeneration is a word that has been used a great deal locally during the last few years. Is Bexhill still a resort, or is it now entirely residential? The economy of the town, transport links and employment prospects all need to be improved. Historically we have seen that the town has never lacked ambition or innovative ideas, although it has frequently been held back by lack of funds, political will and public support. The future of the De La Warr Pavilion is vital to the image of the town and the Museum is necessary to preserve its heritage. Does the town's future lie with Hastings, and if so can Bexhill retain its own identity? It is noteworthy that an amalgamated Rother District Council and Hastings Borough Council would cover an area roughly approximating to the ancient Hæstingas tribal area.

Appendix One

KING OFFA'S CHARTER OF AD 772 (INVERSION CORRECTED)

†In the name of our Lord God and Saviour. What is done for the present world barely lasts until death, but what is done for eternal life remains forever after death. Therefore it is for everyone with deep forethought of mind to ponder and consider how, with the fleeting possessions of this world, they may obtain for their treasure the dwellings of heavenly promise.

Wherefore I, Offa, King of the English, for the good of my soul and for the love of God, grant everlasting possession to the venerable Bishop Oswald of a certain piece of land in Sussex in fulfilment of a former promise to Almighty God, to build there a monasterium church augmenting the basilica, that can be seen to serve and praise God and honour the Saints, that is the eight cassatos in the locality known as Bixlea. The aforesaid aims are thus realized.

These are eight hides relating to the inland of the land of the Bexware - first to the servants tree - from the servants tree eastward and up to the old marsh dyke - then south to the treacherous place - along the strand over against Codan cliff - north to Kayworth and to the bending stream - north through Shortwood to the landmark beacon - from the beacon to the haunted ford - from the ford along the water to the street bridge - from the bridge up along the drainage ditch to the bedan pool - from the pool south along the boundary thus to the servants tree.

These are outlands that pay tribute to Bexlea. In the locality known by these names: at Barnhorn 3 hides, at Worsham 1, at Ibbanhurst 1, at Crowhurst 8, at the Ridge 1, at Gyllingham 2, at Foxham and Black Brooks 1, at Icklesham 3. With fields, woods, meadows, fisheries and all things pertaining thereto.

Let the aforesaid land remain from this day given as I have said for me in the name of God, free from all royal exaction and bound to the use of those serving God, but on this condition, that after this day, this gift be returned to the episcopal see that is called Selsey. If anyone at any time in greater or lesser degree dares to reduce this gift made by me, let him know that he will incur the penalty for his presumption in the stern judgement of the all-powerful God, and will not escape from a bad hearing.

These are the outspread bounds of Icolesshamme - at the bin well by the cliff - out to the middle of the brookland - to the isolated tatting wood - out onto the moor - to the eadwining valley and the boundary of the Cantware - west along the Bedle brookland middlewards.

This charter was written in the year 772 from the incarnation of our Lord Jesus Christ, on the 10th of the indiction and the 15th day of the month of August.

I, Offa, King of the Mercians, in accord with the power conceded to me by God who reigns, confirm this charter of gift, signing it with my own hand, and placing the sign of the cross.

+ I, Ecberht, King of Kent, have agreed and signed.

+ I, Jaenberht, archbishop by grace of God have signed.

+ I, Cynewulf, King of the West Saxons, have agreed and signed this gift.

+ I, Eadberht, bishop, have agreed and signed.

+ I, Oswald, bishop, have signed this gift made to me.

+ I, Righeah, bishop, have agreed.

+ I, Diora, bishop, have signed.

+ I, Oswald, alderman of the South Saxons, have agreed.

+ I, Osmund, alderman, have confirmed.

+ I, Ælbwald, alderman, have acquiesced.

+ I, Oslac, alderman, have signed.

These witnesses were also present: + Botwine, abbot, + Eata, + Heahberht, + Brorda, + Berhtwald, + Esne, + Huithyse, + Baldraed, + Bryne, + Stidberht, + Cyne, + Ealdraed, + Lulling, + Berht, + Brynhere, + all of the shire, + Æmele, prefect.

This is the land relating to Barnhorn - first at the moss well - from the well south and east to the old road - and the road to the landmark beacon that stands on the east side of the road - to the deep valley and the rush pond - from the pond north to the black stream - up and along the stream to Swineham - south to the sewer and along the stream to Picknill - south by the eastern moor and horn - east to the yew dish - north to the wood and east along the wood.

South to the valley - up on the little heath feld - to the goblin well - south to cyllan mount - from the mount to the cyllan well - west along the stream to Thunor's lair - along the western stream abutting the salt marsh to the fiveways - north along the moor to the place of slaughter and the northern foul water ford - up the old dyke - east along the dyke and thus to the moss well.

Note: The charter is written partly in Latin and partly in Old (Anglo-Saxon) English. Old English text is shown in italics. The 'Servants Tree' was probably a wayside cross, set up by church personnel.

Compiled by Mr William Hedger.

Appendix Two

LORDS AND LADIES
OF THE MANOR

1570   Thomas Sackville, Lord Buckhurst. Created Earl of Dorset in 1604. Granted the Manor of Bexhill by Queen Elizabeth I.

1608   Henry Sackville. Thomas Sackville left the Manor of Bexhill to his younger son Henry, with reversion to Robert, eldest son and heir. Henry died within a few months and his brother Robert died in 1609. Henry also owned the Manor of Cooden that had been acquired by Sir Richard Sackville, his grandfather.

1608   Robert Sackville, 2nd Earl of Dorset. Eldest son of Thomas.

1609   Richard Sackville, 3rd Earl of Dorset. Eldest son of Robert.

1624   Edward Sackville, 4th Earl of Dorset. Brother of Richard.

1652   Richard Sackville, 5th Earl of Dorset. Son of Edward, Richard had married Frances Cranfield, daughter and wealthy heiress of Lionel Cranfield, Earl of Middlesex.

1677   Frances, Countess of Dorset. Frances is mentioned as Lady of the Manor only in the Bexhill Manor Court records of 1678. In 1679 she married secondly Henry Powle, Master of the Rolls. From 1679 until 1687, the year of her death, Bexhill Court records mention neither a Lord nor a Lady of the Manor.

1688   Richard Sackville. Younger son of the 5th Earl. Held Bexhill Manor until 1694.

1695   Charles Sackville, 6th Earl of Dorset. Eldest son of the 5th Earl. He had been created Earl of Middlesex and Baron Cranfield in 1675. These titles then descended with that of Dorset, which he had inherited in 1677.

1706   Lionel Sackville, 7th Earl of Dorset. Created Duke of Dorset in 1720. Son of the 6th Earl and his second wife Mary Compton, daughter of the 3rd Earl of Northampton.

1765   George Sackville, commonly called Lord George Sackville. In 1769 he inherited the Germain estate of Drayton and from 1770 assumed the name of Lord George Germain. George was the third and youngest son of Lionel, the 1st Duke of Dorset, who bequeathed the Manor of Bexhill to him for life. Soldier, politician and Secretary of State for the American Colonies, he achieved notoriety when, as a commander of the British forces at the Battle of Minden, he was said to have disobeyed orders. He incurred the wrath of King George II and was sacked from the army. He did not find favour again until the advent of King George III in 1782; he was created Viscount Sackville of Drayton, but remained known as Lord George Germain.

1785   John Frederick Sackville, 3rd Duke of Dorset. Charles, 2nd Duke of Dorset, eldest son of Lionel, never owned the Manor of Bexhill. John Frederick became 3rd Duke in 1769, but did not gain Bexhill Mnor ownership until 1785. The 3rd Duke was the son of John Sackville, the second son of Lionel.

1799   Arabella Diana, Duchess Dowager of Dorset. The daughter and wealthy heiress of Sir Charles Cope Bt. She married firstly, in 1799, John Frederick, the 3rd Duke, and secondly, in 1801, Lord Whitworth, created Earl Whitworth in 1815. The Bexhill Manor Court Roll refers to her as 'the testamentary guardian lawfully appointed of her only son, the most Noble George Frederick, Duke of Dorset, an infant, and as such Lady of the Manor'.

1814   George John Frederick Sackville, 4th Duke of Dorset. An entry in the Bexhill Manor Court Roll of 1 December 1814 refers for the first and last time to the 4th Duke of Dorset as Lord of the Manor. He died in 1815 aged 21 years, following a fall whilst horse jumping in Ireland. The title passed to his cousin Charles Sackville Germain, who became the 5th and last Duke of Dorset, dying unmarried in 1843. Ownership of the Sackville Estates remained with Arabella Diana, eventually to be inherited by the two daughters of her marriage with the 3rd Duke:

Lady Mary Sackville, following marriage in 1811 Countess of Plymouth.
Lady Elizabeth Sackville, following marriage in 1813 Countess De La Warr.

1815   Charles, Lord Viscount Whitworth and Arabella Diana, Duchess Dowager of Dorset.

1825   Other Archer Windsor, Earl of Plymouth, and Mary, Countess of Plymouth. George John West, Earl De La Warr, and Elizabeth, Countess De La Warr. Subsequent entries in the Court Books omit references to the two ladies.

1829   Other Archer Windsor, 7th Earl of Plymouth. The Sackville Estates had been shared. Mary, Countess of Plymouth inherited the Manor of Bexhill.

1833   Mary, Countess Dowager of Plymouth.

1840   William Pitt, Earl Amherst. Mary had remarried.

1863   Mary, Countess Dowager Amherst.

1865   George John Sackville-West, 5th Earl De La Warr. Mary died without issue. Elizabeth inherited her sister's estates. George John had added 'Sackville' to the family name West in 1843.

1869   Elizabeth, Countess Dowager De La Warr. Created Baroness Buckhurst in 1854, a title that had lapsed with the death of the 5th Duke of Dorset. Her family consisted of six sons and three daughters. The eldest son had died in 1850.

1870   Charles Richard Sackville-West, 6th Earl De La Warr. The second son of the 5th Earl. He never married.

1873   Reginald Windsor Sackville, 7th Earl De La Warr. The third son of the 5th Earl. As second surviving son on the death of his mother in 1870, he had received the title of Baron Buckhurst and the family home of Knole. In 1871 he had abandoned the name of West. The early death of his brother, unmarried, in the river Cam in 1873, brought him the title of 7th Earl De La Warr, and the estate that included the Manor of Bexhill. He had to relinquish possession of Knole, but he kept the title Baron Buckhurst, which was to pass on to his descendents. The long association between Bexhill and the stately home of Knole thus came to an end.*

1895   Gilbert George Reginald Sackville, commonly called Viscount Cantelupe, following the death of his father in 1896, 8th Earl De La Warr. The second son of the 7th Earl De La Warr. The elder son had died in 1890 when his yacht sank in Belfast Lough. The eldest sons of the Earls De La Warr took their father's title of Cantelupe. The 5th Earl was so styled when he married Lady Elizabeth Sackville.

1916   Muriel Agnes, Countess De La Warr. The third daughter of Thomas Brassey, Baron Brassey, had married the 8th Earl in 1891 and divorced him in 1902. She was the mother of his son born in 1900 and thus a minor when his father died in 1915.

1921   Herbrand Edmond Dundonald Brassey Sackville, 9th Earl De La Warr. Prior to the death of his father styled Lord Buckhurst.

*Note:
4th son Mortimer Sackville-West, inherited Knole 1873, created Lord Sackville 1876.
5th son Lionel Sackville-West, became 2nd Lord Sackville 1888.
6th son William Edward Sackville-West, died 1905. His son Lionel, who became 3rd Lord Sackville in 1908, had married Victoria, natural daughter of Lionel 2nd Lord Sackville. The daughter of the marriage, Vita Sackville-West, was to be denied ownership of Knole because of her sex. Possession went to her uncle the 4th Lord Sackville.

Compiled by Mr William Hedger.

124

Appendix Three

POPULATION OF BEXHILL

Year	Population	Inhabited Houses
1801	1091	180
1811	1627	263
1821	1907	311
1831	1931	372
1841	1916	411
1851	2148	429
1861	2084	447
1871	2158	456
1881	2452	520
1891	5206	1009
1894	6770	1354
1895	7105	1421
1896	8150	1630
1897	8910	1782
1898	11,000	2047
1899	12,000	2211
1901	12,213	2659
1911	15,330	
1921	20,036	3510
1931	21,229	4911
1941	No census due to war	
1951	25,668	
1961	28,941	
1971	32,898	13,755
1981	34,772	
1991	38,905	
2001	40,495	

Appendix Four

Martello Towers
in Bexhill

Tower	Location and Notes	Disappeared
44	Galley Hill. Later addition (built *c.*1808/9). The only Bexhill tower to be surrounded by a moat.	1868
45	Sackville Hotel, De la Warr Parade – First Bexhill tower to disappear – lost to the sea.	1822
46	The Colonnade. The site was originally known as 'The Horn'. Traces of the tower were found in 1910 when the Colonnade was built.	1866
47	Sited on a small promontory seawards of the present day Royal Sovereign Café. Vulnerable to high tides it had to be protected from the sea.	1859
48	Sited near the eastern end of South Cliff, south of today's Southcourt Road.	1865
49	Sited at the end of the low cliffs south of Hartfield Road. Probably the Cooden tower used 1860 as a target for an artillery demonstration.	1862
50	A little westward of today's Cooden Beach Hotel. 'The Bricks' Coastguard shelter is thought to have been built with remains.	
51	Sited on a low cliff at Culvercroft Bank, about 200 yards east of the Cooden fishing boat stade. Fell into the encroaching sea.	1869
52	Alongside the present-day East stream discharge outfall, a site now covered by the sea at high tide.	1870/1899
53	East of a then much longer eastern Wallers Haven outfall reservoir.	1870/1899
54	West of the now obsolete Wallers Haven western outfall. Shows on 1909 OS 25" map, sheet 70/9.	1914
55	South-east of Rockhouse Bank.	Survives

In 1909 the sites of towers 53, 54 and 55, were sold by the War Department to private buyers (with towers 54 and 55), and laid out in building plots,

The Bexhill census of 1841, and that of 1851, show that most of the towers were used to accommodate Coastguard personnel and their families. They included many children.

Coastguard stations were later built at Galley Hill, The Colonnade, Cooden Beach (then known as Kewhurst), and adjoining the Wallers Haven outfalls at Normans Bay where the old Coastguard cottages still exist.

Compiled by William Hedger.

Appendix Five

BEXHILL BOROUGH MAYORS

1902–1903	Ebenezer Howard
1903–1905	Gilbert George Reginald Sackville,
	8th Earl De La Warr
1905–1906	Daniel Mayer
1906–1907	James Mackey Glover
1907–1908	Thomas Brassey
	(Baron Brassey, later 1st Earl Brassey)
1908–1909	Thomas Allnutt Brassey
	(Viscount Hythe, later 2nd Earl Brassey)
1909–1911	John Alexander Paton
1911–1914	Daniel Mayer
1914–1916	Frank Bond
1916–1918	Joseph Barker Wall
1918–1920	George Herbert Gray
1920–1921	James Gibb
1921–1922	Arthur George Wells
1922–1923	Ronald Gibb CBE
1923–1924	Ernest William Bowrey
1924–1925	Richard Cecil Sewell
1925–1926	Frank Bausor Bending
1926–1927	Sir Ernest Birch KCMG
1927–1928	William Herbert Mullens DL, JP
1928–1930	Alexander Turner Laing
1930–1932	Christine Isabella Meads
1932–1935	Herbrand Edward Dundonald Brassey Sackville,
	9th Earl De La Warr
1935–1936	Oscar Striedinger CBE, DSO

1936-1942	William Nicholson Cuthbert JP
1942-1943	Frederick Foster Wimshurst
1943-1944	William Howard Hughes
1944-1946	Ernest William Bowrey
1946-1947	Samuel John Taylor
1947-1948	William Howard Hughes
1948-1949	William Howard Hughes
1949-1951	Claude Pycroft MB, ChB
1951-1953	Gilbert Harry Godwin
1953-1954	Granville Boyle Coghlan MA
1954-1956	Joyce Oliver Alexander
1956-1958	Edgar Carter
1958-1960	John Baker
1960-1961	Reginald Frank Botting
1961-1962	Frank Ernest Cooper
1962-1963	Joyce Oliver Alexander
1963-1964	Eric Henry Corke
1964-1965	Allan Sidney John Stevens
1965-1966	Ernest Thomas Robinson
1966-1967	Margaret Ethel Ackland
1967-1968	John Baker
1968-1969	Eric Trehearne Johnson
1969-1970	William Arthur Sole
1970-1971	Donald Ashley Kimber
1971-1973	William George Sansom
1973-1974	Harold George Morgan

REFERENCES

Chapter 1 – The Beginning

1. Wills, J. Pearce MD, MS, MRCS, *From Bexelei to Bexhill, Being a short account of the history and present condition of Bexhill in Sussex* (St Leonards-on-Sea: Whittaker & Williams, Royal Victoria Library, 1888).
2. Combes, Pamela, and Lyne, Malcolm, 'Hastings, Haestingaceaster and Hastingaport. A Question of Identity' *Sussex Archaeological Collections*, vol. 133, 1995.
3. Straker, Ernest, *Wealden Iron* (The Whitefriar Press Ltd, 1931).

Chapter 2 – Lordship of the Church

1. Brandon, Peter (ed.), *The South Saxons* (Phillimore & Co. Ltd, 1978), pp.33-4.
2. Stenton, Sir Frank, *Anglo-Saxon England* (Oxford, 1971), p.208.
3. Barker, Eric, 'Sussex Anglo-Saxon Charters', *Sussex Archaeological Collections*, vol. 86, 1947, pp.90-5.
4. Gardiner, Mark, 'Some lost Anglo-Saxon charters and the endowment of Hastings College', *Sussex Archaeological Collections*, vol. 127, 1989, p.45.
5. Morris, John (ed.), *Domesday Book, Sussex* (Phillimore, 1976), f.18b-18b,c.
6. *Chichester Chartulary* (Sussex Records Society Volume 46), p.15.
7. 'Some lost Anglo-Saxon charters', p.46.
8. *Chichester Chartulary*, p.14.

Chapter 3 – Lordship of the Sackville Family

1. Mullens, William Herbert, *A Short History of Bexhill* (privately published, Bexhill 1927), p.15.

Chapter 4 – Coal Mining, Soldiers and Smugglers

1. Torrens, H.S., 'Coal Hunting in Bexhill', *Sussex Archaeological Collections*, vol. 136, 1998, pp.177-91.
2. *The King's German Legion from Bexhill to the Battle of Waterloo*, The Bexhill Hanoverian Study Group, 2003.
3. *Sussex Archaeological Collections*, vol. 54, p.86.

Chapter 6 – The 8th Earl De La Warr

1. *The Hooley Book, the amazing financier: his career and his 'crowd'*, anon, 1904.

Chapter 7 – The 9th Earl and the De La Warr Pavillion

1. Milligan, Spike, *Adolf Hitler: My Part In His Downfall* (Penguin Books Ltd, 1971).
2. Armstrong, Noel F., *Sussex Witchcraft* (James Pike Ltd, 1976), p.20.
3. *Ibid.* p.32.

INDEX

Numbers in **bold** refer to page numbers of illustrations